COOL CAREERS WITHOUT COLLEGE FOR
PEOPLE
WHO LOVE
VIDEO
GAMES

COOL CAREERS WITHOUT COLLEGE FOR
PEOPLE
WHO LOVE
VIDEO
GAMES

NICHOLAS CROCE

The Rosen Publishing Group, Inc., New York

Published in 2007 by The Rosen Publishing Group, Inc.
29 East 21st Street, New York, NY 10010

Library of Congress Cataloging-in-Publication Data

Croce, Nicholas.
Cool careers without college for people who love video games/Nicholas Croce.
    p. cm.—(Cool careers without college)
Includes index.
ISBN 1-4042-0747-3 (library binding)
1. Video games-Vocational guidance-Juvenile literature. I. Title. II. Series.
GV1469.3.C65 2006
794.8023-dc22

                                                              2005028742

Manufactured in the United States of America

CONTENTS

INTRODUCTION

A video game is essentially a complex, dynamic, and interactive piece of visual art. Video games, currently a $10 billion business, are hotter than they have ever been. New technologies, more exciting plotlines, and greater promotion are all helping the industry become one of the hottest markets around. For this reason, learning about the jobs that are available in this field is an important step in potentially securing a highly successful career down the road.

Video games have become such big business that organized conventions are arranged for companies to show off their latest games and products. Here, gamers are trying out Microsoft's Xbox console at the 10th annual Electronic Entertainment Expo (E³), the world's largest video game convention.

In this book, you will be introduced to and will learn about a variety of careers in the video game industry that do not require a college degree. It is a challenging field, however, and requires determination, motivation, and hard work.

Regardless of your interests and talents, there is likely a job for you in the industry, whether in game creation or the retail side of selling the finished product. If you like dealing with people, there are jobs that require good social skills, such as video game store salesperson. Are you independent and creative? You might be well suited for starting your own business related to video games, such as online rentals or a retail store. If you are a good artist, you might be interested in animating video game characters. Are computers your thing? Read up on how to become a game programmer. Do you like to write? Most games have story lines, just like books and movies. Writers are needed to think up creative and interesting plots. Or you might like to review video games for a magazine. Finally, if you like to play video games, which you probably do, jobs exist that will pay you to sit in front of a screen and play all day long!

In addition to looking at these careers, chapters offer additional research material related to the jobs covered. These resources include books and Web sites that you can use to further your knowledge and keep up to date on industry trends.

1

STORY WRITER

Have you ever written a poem, play, or story? Do you enjoy novels with intriguing plotlines? Are you interested in complex characters? If so, you may enjoy writing for video games.

Strong character development is playing an increasing role in modern games. Writing takes place extensively at every phase of game development. Writers contribute to the overall story line, as well as the characters' personalities, dialogue, and even names of places.

As games become more complex and lifelike, the demand for talented writers grows. Think back to some games from five or ten years ago. Remember how basic and simple they were? The characters were not very interesting, and the story lines, if there were any at all, were just plain dull. Now think of the games we have today. They are a far cry from story lines such as that of *Pac-Man*, the early 1980s' game in which the objective is for Pac-Man to eat as many dots as he can without being eaten by ghosts. It is easy to see how far story writers for video games have come and how important they are today.

However, don't think that story writing for a video game company means being able to sit and write without interruption all day long. Writers are involved in every step of the process, and their job includes more than just writing. Since many game stories are created collaboratively, writers do a lot of reading and meeting. They read design documents and flow charts. These are documents the game designers create to give writers an initial concept of how the game will look visually. Writers then use these documents to pen story lines around the visual world the designers created. The meeting part of the writers' day is probably the most important since they work frequently

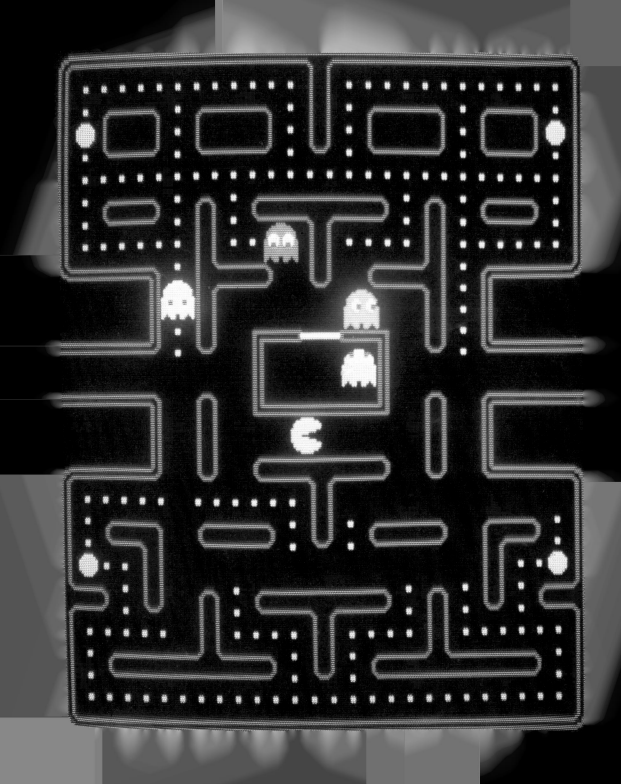

with designers. Because designers are a significant part of the writers' team, it is important to meet with the design department to make sure that everyone is on the same page, so to speak.

Education and Training

You might be thinking, there is no way I can be a writer: writers work for the *New York Times* and have journalism degrees. Don't be discouraged. As long as you enjoy writing and can show a video game company that you have the power of the pen, your chances of becoming a video game story writer are good. Just make sure that this job is right for you. Are you interested in writing? Do you have an excellent grasp of language? Do you know proper spelling and grammar? Is your writing interesting?

Writing is a good position for a person with a vivid imagination. And since most video games are fictional, knowing how to write fiction is also essential. Do you understand the basics of plot structure? You should be able to create three-dimensional characters who speak lifelike

Video game story lines have advanced greatly since the days of *Pac-Man* in the early 1980s. The game's goal was simple: to have Pac-Man eat as many white dots as possible without getting eaten himself. Today, video game story lines can be as involved and far-reaching as saving the world and all humankind.

dialogue. You should also be able to evoke emotion and build tension by including suspenseful situations. These are all talents that good writers have. It is also helpful to read screenplays, study film writing, and familiarize yourself with basic storytelling techniques, especially with those used in game design.

Salary

Though writing is becoming an ever more important job in video game development, it is still rare to have a full-time in-house job as a writer at a video game company. Most writers work as freelancers, which means they take on projects as they become available. This also means that rather than earning a yearly salary, writers usually get paid by the hour. As an entry-level writer, you can expect to earn about $30 an hour. Depending on how many projects you have, you can make up to $60,000 a year. More experienced writers command more money, up to $60 an hour. With this hourly rate and constant work, you can make up to $120,000 a year. The trick with freelancing, though, is being able to find enough work to keep you busy all the time, as there might not always be projects available.

Outlook

In terms of the respect it gets from the industry, the story writer career is still in its infancy. As games become more complex and lifelike, the writing is also going to have to improve. For you, this means more creative and financial opportunities. By landing a job as a story writer now, you can advance as writers continue to become more in demand.

The Story Line for *Halo 2*

With most video games, you spend all your time behind the controls rather than paying attention to the story line. But the story behind the game is really where all the action takes place. For the game *Halo 2*, the Master Chief, the hero commander of the game, is on a mission to save Earth. Master Chief's job is to fight the Covenant, an alien alliance that has just arrived on Earth and is out to destroy the world. With the help of a fleet of marines, Master Chief defends Earth from the Covenant warship and eventually finds himself inside its confines. To find out what happens to Master Chief once inside the enemy ship, you'll just have to play for yourself!

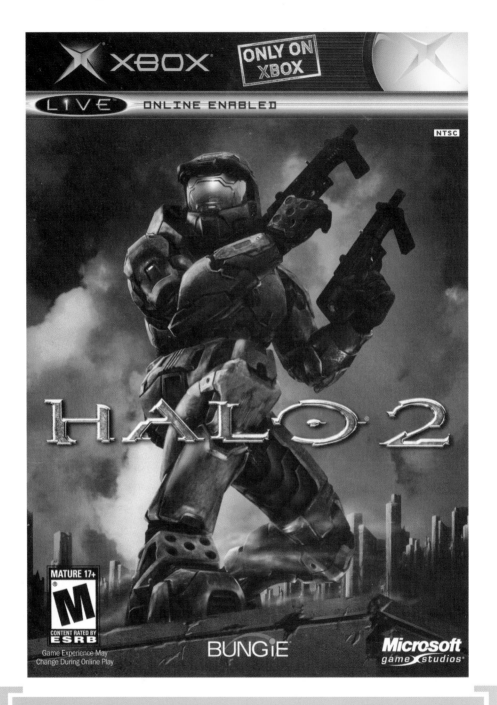

Halo 2 has been one of the best-selling games of all time. In 2004, it was the second-best-selling game of the year, selling 4.2 million copies in the United States between its release in November and the end of the year. The success of Halo 2 has almost certainly resulted from its complex and interesting story line.

FOR MORE INFORMATION

ORGANIZATIONS

Canadian Authors Association (CAA)

National Office
Box 419
Campbellford, ON K0L 1L0
Canada
(866) 216-6222 or (705) 653-0323
Web site: http://www.canauthors.org

The CAA slogan, "Writers Helping Writers," lives up to its promise. This national organization has local branches that provide members with services, publications, a members-only listserv, and the ability to network with other aspiring and professional writers.

National Writers Union

113 University Place, 6th Floor
New York, NY 10003
(212) 254-0279
Web Site: http://www.nwu.org

The National Writers Union is a member of the AFL-CIO, the union conglomerate that protects the rights of workers. It is the only union that represents freelance writers of all genres, formats, and media.

The Writers' Center

4508 Walsh Street
Bethesda, MD 20815
(301) 654-8664
Web site: http://www.writer.org

The Writers' Center is a nonprofit organization of writers who support one another's literary creations.

Writers Guild of America, West
7000 West Third Street
Los Angeles, CA 90048
(800) 548-4532
Web Site: http://www.wga.org
> The Writers Guild of America is dedicated to protecting all types of writers and the works they produce. This is a good organization to contact after you have written something and you would like to find out how to register a copyright for it.

The Writers' Union of Canada
90 Richmond Street East, Suite 200
Toronto, ON M5C 1P1
Canada
(416) 703-8982
Web site: http://www.writersunion.ca
> This national organization, which helps Canadian authors protect their works, also brings writers together to help them find work and get published. This is an invaluable resource for both aspiring and professional writers.

WEB SITES

Prima Games
http://www.primagames.com
> Prima Games is among the largest publishers of video game strategy guides. Strategy guides outline the plotlines of a game and how to win.

Xbox.com: Game Detail Page
http://www.xbox.com/en-US/kingdomunderfireheroes/
20050918-fe.htm
> One of the most complex and innovative video game story lines is that of *Kingdom Under Fire: Heroes*. On this official site for Xbox, you will find an outline of the story, from which you can learn what makes for interesting plots, characters, and themes.

BOOKS

Gee, James Paul. *What Video Games Have to Teach Us About Learning and Literacy.* New York, NY: Palgrave Macmillan, 2004.
Gee tells us that video games teach players important world skills, partly because of their story lines. This is an excellent book to see what makes for a good, and educational, video game plot.

Kent, Steven L. *The Ultimate History of Video Games: From Pong to Pokemon—The Story Behind the Craze That Touched Our Lives and Changed the World.* New York, NY: Three Rivers Press, 2001.
This book chronicles the history of the video game industry and gives a good sense of how video game story lines have evolved over the years. From simple *Pac-Man* to the action-packed adventure games of today, this book will give you a panoramic view of video game plot.

Wolf, Mark J. P. *The Video Game Theory Reader.* Oxford, England: Routledge, 2003.
With the popularity of video games exploding, scholars are beginning to analyze video games for their literary and social significance. This book provides insight into what researchers are focusing on in terms of video game story lines and themes.

PERIODICALS

Writer's Digest
4700 E. Galbraith Road
Cincinnati, OH 45236
(513) 531-2222
http://www.writersdigest.com
Writer's Digest magazine is an authority on creative writing. Geared to aspiring writers, the Web site offers tips on what makes a good plotline, how to develop interesting characters, and how to get paid for your work.

2

DESIGNER

Unlike the writer, whose job is to create the thematic structure of a game, the designer is master of everything that is visual in the video game's world. The background, the objects, and the characters in a game are all thought up and created by designers. A game designer is sort of the renaissance person of the development team. A creative

Video game design has become one of the most sought-after fields in the industry. Here, students are taking a course in game design at New York University's Center for Advanced Digital Applications, a non-degree, continuing-education program. Continuing-education programs across the country now commonly offer classes in game creation.

mind, ability to communicate and work well with others, and some writing and artistic talent all contribute to the required skill set. Programming is not a necessity, but you should understand how computer programs work.

There are several things to think about, though, before pursuing a career as a game designer. The job is extremely competitive and highly demanding. It is one of the most sought-after jobs in the industry, so it won't be easy landing a position. Securing your job might be hard, but it is not impossible. Another point to consider is that as a game designer, you won't actually spend the majority of your time designing. In fact, you will probably spend, at most, about 20 percent of your days sitting at a computer designing games. The bulk of your time will be spent imagining the concept for the game, collaborating with the writers to create the game's rules, describing the elements of the game, communicating this information to your colleagues, and keeping the game's vision on track. In other words, as a game designer, you'll need more than just creative talent. You must have good managerial, communication, and technical skills as well.

So what exactly do game designers do? Basically, they are the ones who take the initial story line of a game, originated by the writers, and make it into a real working video game. They construct the backdrop. They also create how

It is important for game designers to be artistic since they draw initial game concepts. Designers sketch out the atmosphere, objects, and character likenesses (such as the one shown here) to present to other members of the team.

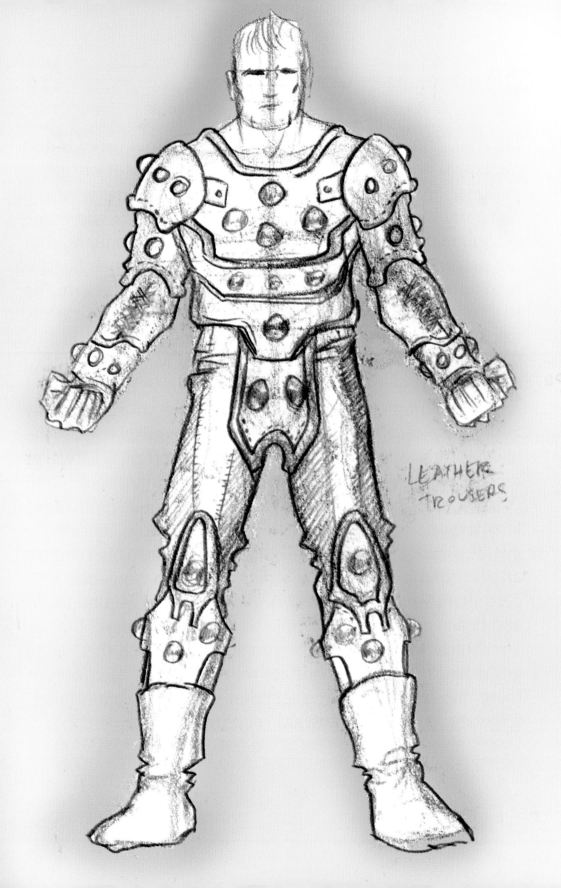

LEATHER
TROUSERS

the characters appear, including how they look, speak, and move. According to Ernest Adams, a veteran game designer, in his book *Break into the Game Industry*, "If the company were designing Monopoly, it would be the game designer who says, 'The board is going to be a [square] that the players go around and around, with properties distributed around it. When a player stops on a property, he has to pay rent to the owner, or he can buy the property from the bank if it's not yet owned by someone.'" In this way, the designer is responsible for the overall concept of the game, as well as its specific rules.

Considering that game designers have to juggle many things, let's see if the job may be right for you. Of course, the obvious first question you should ask yourself is if you're artistic. Though actual designing takes up only about a fifth of a game designer's total duties, artistic abilities are needed in all aspects of the job. Remember, the game designer's day involves imagining the concept of the game. This requires artistic input. Also, are you a people person, someone who gets along well with others? A game designer is a manager and heads up a team of people who conduct different tasks. You'll have to be able to communicate well with this varied group and resolve any conflicts that may arise. Ask yourself these questions and if you feel that you have what it takes, forge ahead and work toward securing that job.

Video game design involves working with a varied team of experts including animators, programmers, and story writers. An early part of the design process is called storyboarding, which presents an idea of how the game will look using a series of rough sketches.

Education and Training

As with many jobs in the video game industry, experience is more respected than education. To land a job as a game designer, you'll need to prove to your potential employer that you have what it takes. This involves showing a body of work, or a portfolio, of what you have done in the past.

You might be saying, how can I get job experience if experience is required to land my first job? This is a valid question and there are two answers. First, to get ahead of your competition, teach yourself about game design. It is also helpful to practice using the software programs needed for game design. The alternative is to land a job at a more entry-level position of level designer. A level designer builds the missions, or levels, that make up a game. This is a basic form of game design and it is a great way to gain the experience necessary to work your way up to the job of game designer.

Salary

Since game designers are so important to the functionality and quality of video games, they are paid relatively well in the industry, and there is plenty of room to grow. As a level designer, you can expect to make anywhere from $40,000 to $55,000 a year. More established designers, or people with the title of game designer, usually make anywhere from $50,000 to $65,000 a year. The next level up from game designer is creative director. People in this position can make $80,000 to $110,000 a year.

Outlook

The explosion in the number of innovative video games makes the job of game designer a great position to be in at the moment. Since game designers have significant influence in the overall concept of the game, their importance and salaries, respectively, are growing. With groundbreaking

A Day in the Life of a Game Designer

So, do you think the job of a game designer sounds interesting and wonder how a designer might spend his or her day? This is what happens during an average day for ubi.com design specialist Patricia Pizer, as explained in *Break into the Game Industry* by Ernest Adams.

Once Pizer gets to work, she answers e-mails and any questions from coworkers. Then she checks Web sites related to any particular game she is working on. After that, she attends a lot of meetings. Pizer usually meets with artists, programmers, and quality assurance specialists. Then she maintains and reviews design specifications. These need constant attention so that the game testers know what potential problems to look for while testing a game.

Pizer also does a lot of research. This research could be related to any game she is working on at the moment, from information on user interface design to anthropology. She also plays games, which is considered research in Pizer's line of work. By playing games, she learns what other designers have done.

games such as the *Grand Theft Auto* series, which required the development of a movielike virtual world, game designers are seeing an increase in the amount of respect they command from their peers.

FOR MORE INFORMATION

ORGANIZATIONS

Entertainment Software Association (ESA)
575 7th Street NW, Suite 300
Washington, DC 20004
Web site: http://www.theesa.com
  The ESA is one of the premiere organizations of video game publishers and manufacturers, with 90 percent of video game software sold in the United States being created by its members. The site includes a PDF document titled "Essential Facts About the Computer and Video Game Industry," which lists other related organizations and can be used as a gateway to additional research.

Full Sail: School of Film, Art, Design, Music & Media Productions
3300 University Boulevard
Winter Park, FL 32792
(800) 226-7625
Web site: http://www.fullsail.com/index.cfm/fa/landing.videogame/mnc/25/video-game
  Though you don't need a college degree for game design, every bit of education helps. Full Sail is a secondary school featuring multimedia education, focusing on game design and development. At

this site, you can learn how to apply to Full Sail as well as general information about the industry itself.

GDIAC: The Game Design Initiative at Cornell University

Department of Computer Science
4130 Upson Hall
Cornell University
Ithaca, NY 14853-7501
(607) 255-7316
Web site: http://www.cs.cornell.edu/projects/game

> Cornell University is one of America's most prestigious institutions. The Game Design Initiative is a listing of courses on game design that are taught at the university as well as a compilation of resources related to the field.

University of Advancing Technology

2625 West Baseline Road
Tempe, AZ 85283-1056
(800) 658-5744
Web Site: http://www.gamedegree.com

> This site provides information on courses available as well as general information on securing a game job. A helpful resource whether you are interested in taking courses in game design or just want to learn more about your opportunities.

WEB SITES

Fabjob.com: Become a Video Game Designer

http://www.fabjob.com/video.html

> FabJob.com is the Web site of a book publishing company whose titles focus on finding careers you enjoy. The FabJob.com Video Game Designer page offers some helpful information related to finding a job in the design area.

Stanford University: History of Video Game Design
http://www.stanford.edu/class/sts145
    This site from Stanford University provides information on video game design and applications for secondary courses on the history of game design.

Washington State University Vancouver: The Art of Computer Game Design
http://www.vancouver.wsu.edu/fac/peabody/game-book/
    Coverpage.html
    This site, hosted by Professor Sue Peabody of Washington State University, features excerpts from the 1982 classic *The Art of Computer Game Design*. The book was written by Chris Crawford, a veteran video game designer, and its excerpts cover areas such as game design sequence, techniques, and tricks.

BOOKS

Bartle, Richard. *Designing Virtual Worlds.* Berkeley, CA: New Riders, 2003.
    This book goes a step further than most in game design instruction by covering the design process of virtual worlds. The author, a renowned expert in game design, guides readers through the complex and fascinating discipline.
Crawford, Chris. *Chris Crawford on Game Design.* Berkeley, CA: New Riders, 2003.
    Chris Crawford is one of today's most sought-after experts in game design. In this book, he explains the fundamental skills required for excellence in the field.
Facts on File, Inc. *Ferguson's Careers in Focus: Computer & Video Game Design.* New York, NY: Facts on File, Inc., 2005.
    This book, geared toward young-adult readers, offers practical and comprehensive advice on all aspects of breaking into a game-design career. From selecting a discipline to choosing secondary education in design, this book is perfect for the novice designer.

Fullerton, Tracy, Christopher Swain, and Steven Hoffman. *Game Design Workshop: Designing, Prototyping, and Playtesting Games*. San Francisco, CA: CMP Books, 2004.
Arguably the best "how to" book on game design, this book is based on a class taught at the University of Southern California. It provides step-by-step instructions and exercises, and includes sidebars from successful game designers.

Olesky, Walter. *Coolcareers.com: Video Game Designer*. New York, NY: The Rosen Publishing Group, Inc., 2000.
This book is a good starting point for anyone interested in a career in game design. It explains in comprehensive language what it takes to become a game designer as well as what to expect once a career is secured.

Rouse, Richard, III. *Game Design: Theory and Practice*. Plano, TX: Wordware Publishing, Inc., 2001.
This multimedia offering comes with book and CD-ROM. The book covers essential game design elements such as game balancing, storytelling, and artificial intelligence. The CD-ROM contains more than a dozen software packages to get started in game design.

Salen, Katie, and Eric Zimmerman. *Rules of Play: Game Design Fundamentals*. Cambridge, MA: MIT Press, 2003.
Bridging different varieties of games, from video games to board games, the authors provide a comprehensive introduction to general game design and what makes for effective design methods. This book guides readers through the connections game design has with the design of much older and tested media.

3

ANIMATOR

Every detail of the backgrounds, characters, and objects within a video game has been created by an animator, who is also known as a production artist. If you are a good artist, enjoy playing video games, and have a facility with computer software, becoming a video game animator might be the goal for you.

Joseph Saulter, founder of Urban Video Game Institute, demonstrates a new version of the company's 3-D animation software. Software programs designed for video game animation are getting better by the day. As these programs improve, the video games themselves become more lifelike and fun.

There's a lot more to the video game animation job, however, than simply animating objects and characters on a screen. Animation is one of the more involved tasks in video game development and requires many skills in addition to artistic ability. As an animator, you will be working with many different types of computer files. These files contain still images, textures, three-dimensional (3-D) models, and two-dimensional (2-D) and 3-D animations, which all work together to compose the seamless flow of play in the final video game product. Though you won't necessarily be creating all these files yourself, you will be working with other artists, designers, and programmers. You will also be teaming up with sound engineers, who will add sound effects, giving your work a more complete and realistic feel.

The process of creating the visual component of the video game is called the production pipeline, and it includes a number of people who work together in various roles. The first step in the process is called concept art and usually includes design of the game characters and the environments in which they exist. Then teams of artists are assigned

Since video game characters are designed to appear as lifelike as possible, the animation process is quite detailed. In this character's 3-D model you can see that every contour of the body is addressed. With this "skeleton" in place, the animator can position the figure in countless ways.

to different aspects of implementing the concept. One group focuses on designing, modeling, and animating the characters. Another team will make 3-D models. If you are creating the quarterback in a football video game, for example, you would begin to implement the character's features and build, using 3-D software tools. You would create the bone structure of the quarterback, called the armature. The armature is basically the video game skeleton of the character, and it guides how the character will move when in motion. Around the armature, a modeler creates the surface. In the quarterback's case, the surface would be his skin, uniform, and helmet. Getting the right surface look is the hardest part. Animators, often a different group from modelers, have to think about such details as how the quarterback will run and what he would look like if he fell to the ground. This is why the job requires a lot of artistic talent. Additionally, there may be some animation elements that require programming, and the animator will often have to integrate these programs into the animation.

Part of the process of creating a video game character's armature is to have an actual person participate in an animation image-capturing session. Here, New England Patriots quarterback Tom Brady wears an outfit with sensors positioned around his body. The movement of these sensors is recorded by a computer, which helps create lifelike action for a football video game.

Though the daily life of an animator or modeler can be challenging and involve long hours, it is often also a lot of fun. Since you will be working with other animators and artists, you will learn from and be inspired by one another's work. Animator Michelle Sullivan, of Turbine Entertainment, says in *Break into the Game Industry* that her day often involves giving feedback on other artists' work, giving quick teaching sessions to fellow employees about different animation techniques, and even the occasional Nerf football skirmish!

Despite taking time for Nerf football, animators and modelers are among the most hardworking people in the video game industry, as well as among the most passionate about what they do. If you like the visual arts and have a knack for computer programs, animation may be your best route into the video game world.

Education and Training

If you want to animate, you should be able to draw. Though this sounds obvious, there are a lot of people who think that the computer will create the art for them, making their own artistic ability a less important qualification.

As an animator, you should also be quite proficient with computers. Specifically, you should be familiar with the programs Adobe Photoshop, Adobe Illustrator, Corel Graphics, Maya, and 3D Studio Max. These programs allow you to create and alter images for both 2-D and 3-D animation. It may

Interviewing Tips

No matter what job you are interviewing for, the first encounter with a potential employer can be a nerve-racking experience. One good thing to remember is that your interviewer probably understands that this is a stressful part of the job-application process and will likely not hold it against you if you appear a little nervous. In fact, he or she may even look upon it favorably. When you're nervous, it's often a sign that you care about getting the job.

In any case, here are a few steps you can take to make your interview a more pleasant experience while increasing your chances of getting the job:

- Dress professionally and look confident.
- Arrive a few minutes early.
- Complete your application in detail and be truthful.
- Be polite.
- Smile and be enthusiastic.
- Maintain good posture.
- Ask questions about the position.
- Bring extra copies of your résumé and/or portfolio.

also be handy to have some experience working with a game engine such as Torque, Half-Life, or Unreal.

These computer programs might sound daunting, but with persistent practice, you can learn to use them. Though it is good to have a degree from a qualified animation school, you do not need to attend a university to learn how to become an animator. You can do it on your own. Get ahold of these programs. Once you have them, you can begin testing your artistic creations. Though the programs all have "help" sections and tutorials that guide you through the learning process, your most successful bet is trial and error. There are also many books and online guides to help you along. Play around with the programs and you will soon know your stuff.

Salary

There is a lot of room for growth within the animation field. Entry-level modelers and animators earn anywhere from $25,000 to $35,000 a year. As you move up the ladder to mid-level artist, you can expect to make from $40,000 to $75,000 a year. The top-level artist, called an art director, can command a salary of $80,000 to $125,000 a year.

Outlook

Video game graphics are becoming more and more detailed and lifelike, so demand for talented modelers and animators is growing every day. In addition, because of ever-improving visual effects, video games are increasingly being accepted as mainstream media. Major companies frequently advertise their products in video games, and video games are even starting to be advertised in movie theaters. This focus on games as a significant medium makes the animator's job that much more important.

FOR MORE INFORMATION

ORGANIZATIONS

ACM SIGGRAPH
G. Scott Owen, President
Department of Computer Science
Georgia State University
Atlanta, GA 30309
(714) 781-3921
Web site: http://www.siggraph.org
> ACM SIGGRAPH is a nonprofit organization dedicated to promoting information related to computer graphics and interactive techniques, including video game animation.

IEEE Computer Society
1730 Massachusetts Avenue NW
Washington, DC 20036-1992
(202) 371-0101
Web site: http://www.computer.org
> The IEEE Computer Society is the largest organization of computer professionals in the world. Its Web site includes career development and job sections, and a digital library of publications, including *IEEE Computer Graphics and Applications*.

WEB SITES

About.com: Computer Animation for Video Games

http://animation.about.com/od/videogameanimation

A Web site that provides information on video game animation as well as a list of other useful sites.

ADigitalDreamer.com: Animation Career Information

http://www.adigitaldreamer.com/articles/animationcareerinfo.htm

This site provides information on what it takes to break into an animation career and offers advice on the different paths one can take within the industry.

Animation Arena: Video Game Design

http://www.animationarena.com/video-game-design-articles.html

The numerous articles provided on this site cover topics on video game design and animation. Some of the best secondary design schools for video game animation are also listed.

Animation School Review: Video Game Animation Skills

http://www.animationschoolreview.com/game-animation-skills.html

Here you can find a thorough introduction to video game animation and the skills necessary to become successful.

Animation Schools Index

http://www.animationschoolsindex.com

Though you may not be looking for a college degree, secondary school education in game animation is helpful. This site provides a listing of numerous schools that offer education in the field.

Digital Audio Video

http://www.digitalaudiovideo.com/index.php?module=reviews&category=game

This Web site reviews some of the hottest games on the market today.

Herzing College: School of Design: 3-D Animation/Video Games
http://www.herzing.edu/school.php?program=230&campus=19
    The Herzing College Web site provides information on attending secondary classes in video game animation and offers general information on the field.

BOOKS

Bancroft, Tom. *Designing Characters with Personality: For Film, TV, Animation, Video Games, and Graphic Novels.* New York, NY: Watson-Guptill Publications, 2006.
    This book explains how to make characters lively by using techniques mastered by pros in video game animation as well as television and movies.

Evry, Harry. *Beginning Game Graphics.* New York, NY: Muska & Lipman, 2004.
    Those looking to enter the world of video game animation and graphics will find this title to be a good introduction.

Funge, John David. *AI for Computer Games and Animation: A Cognitive Modeling Approach.* Wellesley, MA: A.K. Peters, Ltd., 1999.
    AI, or artificial intelligence, is a component of video games that allows the game to learn on its own, and it is a growing field in video game animation. This book provides an accessible overview.

Menache, Alberto. *Understanding Motion Capture for Computer Animation and Video Games.* San Francisco, CA: Morgan Kaufmann, 1999.
    This book concentrates on a small but important area of animation called motion capture, which is increasingly being used in motion pictures and video games.

Murdock, Kelly L. *3-D Game Animation for Dummies.* Hoboken, NJ: John Wiley & Sons, Inc., 2005.
    A full overview of 3-D animation is offered in an accessible and entertaining manner.

4

PROGRAMMER

Imagine turning on your favorite video game. Let's say it is *MLB 2006*, the popular major league baseball game. The game starts and you *see* the baseball field, the players, and the fans in the stands, but nothing *happens*. All the characters and objects in the game are motionless. You might as well be looking at a painting. This is what would happen if there were no one to program the game. You would have all the basic elements of the game, such as the game's concept, graphics, and sounds, but there would be nothing to link all these elements together and bring the game to life.

Game programmers, however, do more than just link together all the elements of a game. The job requires a lot of technical skill and attention to detail, probably the most out of all the disciplines in the industry. This is because in order to create a program, programmers have to write a very intricate and complex computer language called code. Code is essentially the language that translates a game player's actions to the video game console. For example, if you give the command to your player in *MLB 2006* to swing at a pitch by pressing a certain button, it is the code that tells the game console to make your player swing the bat.

There's more to the job than writing code. Programmers must also test their code and debug, or fix, any problems. Code is often such a complicated language that the slightest mistake can take hours, if not days, to correct. A simple error in code, such as typing >= instead of <=, could create a world of headaches for the programmer.

In addition to sitting in front of a computer writing and testing code, programmers often attend meetings and strategy sessions. Since programming involves coordinating all the elements of a game, programmers need to be in constant communication with other team members, such as artists, designers, writers, and audio specialists.

Programming is an important and complicated job, and there are multiple areas of the discipline in which you can specialize. For example, you can focus on graphics, audio, or security. Among these, graphics is the most popular—and competitive—specialization for programmers. Graphics programming involves writing code for the actual animation of the scenes on the screen. As games grow more advanced, audio programming is also becoming popular. An audio programmer might program the game to include interactive audio, which is provided by the audio specialist, such as a certain type of song queued to play when a specific action in the game is taken. Finally, with hackers growing bolder and wiser in terms of what they are able to break into, security programmers are becoming more important. Security programmers design the game so that it is hard or nearly impossible for hackers to steal the game and distribute it for themselves, for instance on the Internet.

Video game programming involves a lot more than just writing code. Programmer Jeff Dobson demonstrates *Star Wars Galaxies: Jump to Light Speed* at E^3 (the Electronic Entertainment Exposition), in Los Angeles, California. E^3 is the largest video game exposition in the world and an excellent place to get a glimpse of the latest products on the market.

Video gaming has historically been a male-dominated industry, but more women, such as Tammy Yap, seen here, are becoming interested in the field. Game makers are hoping that games created by women will attract more female customers.

Education and Training

You do not need a college education to become a programmer, but you do require a thorough knowledge of computers. To get a job as a programmer, you also often need a good deal of experience with certain computer languages. Among these languages are C, C++, and Java.

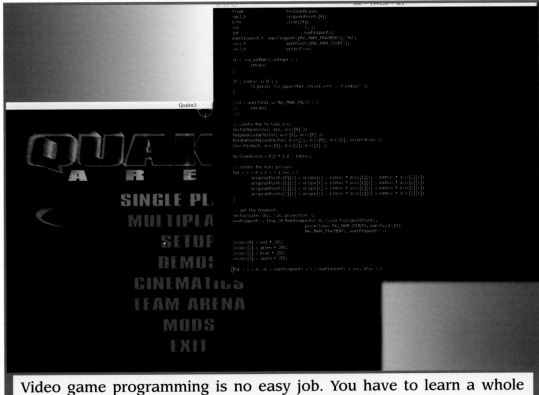

Video game programming is no easy job. You have to learn a whole new language, programming, which is shown here for the video game *Quake III Arena*. What seems like thousands of senseless commands and symbols is really a logical system of directions that the programmer understands.

Salary

Video game programmers have the potential to make a lot of money. Starting out, programmers generally make from $35,000 to $40,000 a year. With several years of experience, however, and proof of programming talent, you can earn anywhere from $50,000 to over $100,000 a year.

Outlook

Out of all the game jobs available, programming is probably in the best place right now. As the expression goes, game programmers are sitting on the nose cone of the rocket. What this means is that programmers are in the position to reach the greatest heights now that the industry is really taking off. Getting into the business now can reap great rewards down the line as more and more complex games gain popularity.

FOR MORE INFORMATION

ORGANIZATIONS
BioWare Corp.
200, 4445 Calgary Trail
Edmonton, AB T6H 5R7
Canada
(780) 430-0164
Web site: http://www.bioware.com
> Bioware, a game manufacturer based in Canada, has an impressive track record. By visiting its Web site, you can search for jobs as well as see just what makes this company successful.

Business Software Alliance

1150 18th Street NW, Suite 700
Washington, DC 20036
(202) 872-5500
Web site: http://www.bsa.org

> The Business Software Alliance helps businesses maintain a safe and legal digital world in terms of protecting software and its users with cybersecurity, e-commerce, and copyright security.

Software & Information Industry Association

1090 Vermont Avenue NW, Sixth Floor
Washington, DC 20005-4095
(202) 289-7442
Web site: http://www.siia.net

> This trade association helps software companies and their employees with business development, software education, and intellectual property (copyright) protection. The Web site's resources include a job network and daily or weekly e-newsletters.

Systems and Software Consortium (SSCI)

2214 Rock Hill Road
Herndon, VA 20170-4227
(703) 742-8877
Web site: http://www.software.org

> SSCI is an organization devoted to keeping its members ahead of the curve in software development. It caters mostly to large businesses, but also to some smaller companies. The organization's Web site provides a wealth of information about membership as well as about the latest software and programming trends.

Ubisoft Canada Inc.
5505 St-Laurent Boulevard, Suite 5000
Montreal, QC H2T 1S6
Canada
(514) 490-2000
Web site: http://www.ubi.com
Ubisoft is a game manufacturer that has produced such hits as *Prince of Persia: The Two Thrones.* The Web site is a great place to gather information on how the business works and how you can advance as a programmer.

WEB SITES
Game Programming Wiki
http://www.gpwiki.org
This site is the definitive source for everything you need to know about game programming. Included is an introduction to what programmers do, tutorials, game ideas, books and reference material, and a community section.

Guru.com: Game Programmer
http://www.guru.com/category.cfm?cid=806&tc=23147&kw=
game%20programmer
Guru.com allows freelancers from all industries to post their work and look for jobs. The game programmer page lets you search for employment or advertise your services.

Open Directory: Computers: Programming: Games
http://dmoz.org/Computers/Programming/Games
This site, maintained by the Open Directory, provides links to hundreds of outside sites related to video game programming.

TheGameCreators.com
http://www.thegamecreators.com
In addition to its products, this site offers information on what tools are available for both beginner and advanced programmers.

Wikipedia.org: Game Programmer
http://en.wikipedia.org/wiki/Game_programmer

This Web encyclopedia page features a variety of game programming information, including the history of programming, required skills, job security, language, and tools.

BOOKS

Davidson, Andrew. *Killer Game Programming in Java.* Sebastopol, CA: O'Reilly Media, Inc., 2005.

Most video games are programmed in the C++ language, but those written in Java are increasing rapidly. This book will teach you everything you need to know about programming in this growing computer language.

Deloura, Mark. *Game Programming Gems.* Florence, KY: Delmar Thomson Learning, 2000.

A book for the game programmer working with C and C++ software. Included are over sixty programming tips compiled by more than forty industry professionals.

Harbour, Jonathan S. *Game Programming All in One.* 2nd ed. New York, NY: Muska & Lipman, 2004.

If you have some knowledge of programming languages such as C and C++, this book is a good next step in honing your game programming skills. Harbour will teach you how to begin to write code that will work on many different platforms.

Sethi, Maneesh. *Game Programming for Teens.* New York, NY: Muska & Lipman, 2003.

If you don't have any experience in game programming, this is the perfect book for you. Written for the novice who wants to break into the industry, the title provides all the basics to create a complete game.

5

AUDIO
SPECIALIST

Do you like music? Do you play an instrument? Are you interested in a wide variety of music? If so, you might want to consider getting involved in video game audio.

Sound is a key part of creating the overall atmosphere of a game. From the simple music behind *Pac-Man* to the colorful soundtracks of modern

The musical score and sound effects are as important to a game as the story line and graphics. Here, the Chicagoland Pops Orchestra performs the soundtrack to the video game *Final Fantasy* in front of a sold-out audience of 4,500 people in Rosemont, Illinois, on February 19, 2005. To heighten the viewing experience, scenes from the game are projected on enormous screens behind the orchestra.

games such as *Halo*, sound effects greatly enhance the overall game-playing experience.

There are several specialized jobs in the audio field, and each requires different talents. One such specialization is Foley editing. Foley editing originated in the movie industry (which goes to show how much video games and movies have in common). In movies, after filming is complete, Foley editors synchronize sounds with the action that's taking

place on screen—think of the sound of the crack of the bat as a baseball player hits a home run. The Foley editor makes sure the sound occurs at the exact moment the ball meets the bat. Foley editors do the same for video games. Going back to our quarterback example, the Foley editor makes sure that the sound of the quarterback getting tackled occurs at the exact moment that it happens on screen.

Another job in the audio field is studio recorder. The studio recorder is the person who gets the sounds that you hear on video games. If the sound needed is someone saying a phrase, for example, the studio recorder will bring an actor into the studio and record the required phrase. This might sound easy, but it can be quite difficult. Over the course of days, one particular phrase may have to be recorded again and again. The actor might sound slightly different from one day to the next. The studio recorder must be able to pick up on this tone variation, so this is a good job for those of you with sharp ears.

Music composition is a third specialization within the audio field. Composers, again much like in the movie industry, create soundtracks for games. This is a much more

> The video game and movie industries use some of the same production practices and techniques, such as Foley editing. They also occasionally share characters. Arnold Schwarzenegger, for example, starred in both the movie and video game versions of *Terminator 3: Rise of the Machines*.

challenging task for games than movies, though, because in games, the scenes and moods, which require different types of music, change at the will of the player. In a movie, the composer knows what's going to happen next. If you have a talent for selecting and composing music that fits a particular mood, music composition might be a good direction for you.

Education and Training

If you want to go into the audio field, you, of course, should have an interest and talent in music. If you want to go into composing, you should be able to read and compose music, and have some basic understanding of music theory. You should also have a firm understanding of computers and computer software since you will be doing most of your work on computers. You will need to be familiar with the software audio professionals use, including waveform editors and MIDI sequencers.

Waveform editor software lets you record and manipulate sounds. Some of the most popular waveform editing software are Pro Tools, Sound Forge, and Peak. MIDI sequencer software takes information about the notes you want to play and puts it all together. It also allows you to manipulate your music in different ways, such as giving it concert-hall quality. Some of the most popular MIDI sequencers are Cubasis, Digital Performer, and SONAR. You can learn how to use these programs on your own, and

Now that popular music is increasingly finding its way into video game soundtracks, audio specialists are beginning to take advantage of music industry recording equipment. Fabrice Dupont, pictured in the foreground, is working with Pro Tools, a music editing software program that is used on 90 percent of the pop music you hear today.

you should have a firm grasp of them before applying for any audio job. Having a background in music doesn't hurt either.

Salary

A good paycheck comes with audio work. In general, audio specialists make between $40,000 and $70,000 a year. Salaries may increase in years to come now that audio is becoming one of the most important features of video games.

The music recording industry, along with Hollywood, has a lot in common with the video game business. Today, game soundtracks are often produced by hit musicians, such as rapper Jermaine Dupri. Dupri, sitting at a studio's mixing board, is shown producing the score for the basketball game *NBA 2K2*.

Outlook

Video games are becoming more and more like other visual media such as television and movies. Companies are beginning to advertise their products on video games. Music companies, too, are starting to pay attention. Games today often feature hit songs by popular artists. The music companies actually pay to advertise their artists' songs in the games. Needless to say, this new form of advertising makes audio jobs that much more important and interesting.

Join a Band

You may not realize it, but if you are a solo musician or member of a band, you may already have a great qualification for being an audio specialist. Musicians use many of the same tools and equipment—microphones, mixers, and equalizers—that audio specialists use. Even better, if you do the sound work for a band, you already have a lot of experience with these devices. If you are not already in a band but have musical talent, you may want to consider joining one. Not only will you gain experience for an audio specialist job, you'll have a lot of fun along the way.

FOR MORE INFORMATION

ORGANIZATIONS

The American Society of Composers, Authors and Publishers
One Lincoln Plaza
New York, NY 10023
(212) 621-6000
Web Site: http://www.ascap.com
> Though not specifically related to audio for video games, this organization is dedicated to protecting the rights and promoting the welfare of all music professionals.

Game Audio Network Guild (G.A.N.G.)
P.O. Box 1001
San Juan Capistrano, CA 92393
(949) 340-3557
Web site: http://www.audiogang.org
> G.A.N.G is a nonprofit organization for interactive audio that supports career development for aspiring game audio professionals, publishers, developers, and students. Registering on the Web site allows you to access all of its resources.

WEB SITES

Interactive Audio Specialist Interest Group (IASIG)
http://www.iasig.org
> IASIG is dedicated to developers of audio software, hardware, and content. The site's goal is to be a virtual community where like-minded audio specialists can exchange ideas and improve the performance of future tools in the audio sector of the industry.

Mark Knight's Game Sounds
http://www.gamesounds.co.uk
> Mark Knight is a video game audio specialist with over eleven years of experience in the industry. On his Web site, Knight offers advice and shows features of projects he's worked on, along with sample downloads. This is a great site to review the accomplishments of a seasoned game audio specialist.

Video Game Audio
http://www.videogameaudio.com
> A site of compiled audio articles by Leonard J. Paul, teacher of video game audio at the Vancouver Film School. The articles cover a broad range of audio-related topics, such as interactive design and teaching audio for games.

BOOKS

Boer, James R. *Game Audio Programming* (Advances in Computer Graphics and Game Development). Boston, MA: Charles River Media, 2002.
A comprehensive guide and good tutorial to audio programming that covers a diverse range of topics, including DirectX audio, decompression libraries, and hardware filters and effects.

Fay, Todd M. *DirectX Audio Exposed: Interactive Audio Development.* Plano, TX: Wordware Publishing, Inc., 2003.
DirectX is Microsoft's game-development program designed for Microsoft Windows operating systems. This book teaches developing video game audio using this reputable program.

Marks, Aaron. *The Complete Guide to Game Audio: For Composers, Musicians, Sound Designers, and Game Developers.* Gilroy, CA: CMP Books, 2001.
This all-encompassing resource for breaking into the audio sector of the video game industry covers subjects such as buying equipment and finding a job.

McCuskey, Mason. *Beginning Game Audio Programming.* New York, NY: Muska & Lipman, 2003.
A book that introduces you to the potential challenges and perks in the world of video game audio. Also included are tips on how to compose dynamic music and 3-D sound.

Sanger, George Alistair. *The Fat Man on Game Audio: Tasty Morsels of Sonic Goodness.* Berkeley, CA: New Riders, 2003.
George "the Fat Man" Sanger introduces readers to the world of video game audio and reveals what it takes to become successful. Sanger understands the intricacies of this area of the industry and offers a much-needed review.

Wasson, Mike, and Peter Turcan. *Fundamentals of Audio and Video Programming for Games.* Redmond, WA: Microsoft Press, 2003.
Published by Microsoft, this book and CD-Rom is an authoritative overview and tutorial of video game audio for C++ computer language programmers.

PERIODICALS

EQ
2800 Campus Drive
San Mateo, CA 94403
(650) 513-4400
Web site: www.eqmag.com
> *EQ* is an audio industry magazine that specializes in news on home recording studio equipment and software. If you want to set up your own studio at home, this is a good resource.

Live Sound International
169 Beulah Street
San Francisco, CA 94117
(415) 387-4009
Web site: http://www.livesoundint.com
> *Live Sound International* is a monthly print and online audio recording industry publication. Sound professionals not only read the magazine, but write the articles. This is a great journal to pick up if you want to learn about the technical details of being an audio specialist.

MIX
745 Fifth Avenue
New York, NY 10151
(212) 745-0100
Web site: http://www.mixonline.com
> *MIX* is a magazine for the professional recording and sound production industry. Articles cover such topics as industry news, profiles of producers and engineers, audio recording, music technology, and production for film and video.

6

PRODUCER

There are three main parts to video game creation. The developer, which is a company (made up of writers, designers, and animators), creates the game in the same way a film company creates a film. The publisher is a company that finances the creation of the game and markets it to the public. A publisher of games is similar to a book publisher, which

Video game producers bring together everyone involved in creating the final product. Gary McKay *(front left)*, Nick Wlodyka *(front center)*, and Bill Harrison *(front right)* make up the production trio that brought together the team that created *FIFA 2002 World Cup Soccer*.

pays the writer to write the book and then markets and sells the book to the public. The final main job of game creation is that of producer. A producer is the middleman between the video game developer and the publisher. It is his or her responsibility to make sure that the game the developer creates reaches the publisher in a timely, efficient, and glitch-free manner. Using the analogy of the book business, a producer is similar to an author's agent, who is the liaison between the author and the publisher.

The job of producer is less creative than other jobs in the game creation industry, such as animator and designer, but it is no less important. In fact, the producer's job is arguably more important than many of the other jobs in the business because without the producer, the game simply would not get made, or "produced," period. In ensuring that the game is properly transferred from the developer to the publisher, the producer is responsible for such tasks as making sure that the quality, timeliness, and budget goals are met; establishing the objectives of the development team; taking care of contracts between the developer and publisher; making sure payments to freelancers are made; interacting with clients; providing status reports to upper management; and managing potential conflicts between team members. Piece of cake, right? Maybe not, but don't be intimidated. Though production is one of the most labor-intensive jobs in the industry, it can also be the most rewarding, as producers are given the respect their hard work deserves.

Since production is such an important and involved job, there are several producer positions, each with its own responsibilities. When starting out, you will likely gain experience at the most entry-level job: associate producer. The associate producer reports directly to the producer. This usually means acting as the assistant to the producer and being responsible for such tasks as helping the producer in the day-to-day management of projects, running errands such as mailing documents, and taking notes at meetings. There are also other, more important tasks the associate producer undertakes, such as researching competitive products and analyzing and testing games in progress.

The next level above associate producer is producer, and then executive producer. The executive producer has a lot of responsibility. Any problems that arise ultimately wind up on the executive producer's desk. The executive producer also oversees all producers working under him or her. In addition, he or she, along with the producer, negotiates contracts between developers and publishers.

Education and Training

Since you will most likely get your foot in the door as an associate producer, the requirement for this position is simply an interest in and general knowledge of video games. However, there are other qualities you will need to last and excel in this field. Since production is foremost a management job, you need to be a people person. You also have to be able to work well under pressure. Production depends heavily on schedules. You will frequently be working under tight deadlines, so you will need to be able to work well

To make sure all aspects of a video game's production stay on track, producers must meet with a variety of people in the industry, from developers and designers to game manufacturers. Since they interact with so many different personalities, it is important that producers have good communication and people skills.

under stressful conditions. In addition, it is important that you be detail oriented. There are a lot of specifics to deal with in the production field, such as tracking dates, addresses, file names, and client contacts. Even tiny mistakes with any of the information could create enormous problems down the line. Are you a people person? Do you thrive under pressure? Are you detail oriented? Great! Becoming a producer might be the right thing for you.

Salary

Since there are different levels of producer, the position has a wide salary range. As an associate producer, you can expect to make anywhere from $40,000 to $70,000 a year. Moving up the ladder to producer, you are looking at a paycheck of anywhere from $50,000 to $70,000 a year. Moving yet higher to executive producer, you could take home anywhere from $75,000 to $95,000 a year. In addition to salary, you will earn the respect and gratification that comes with such an important and involved job.

Outlook

With the growing popularity and complexity of games, the producer's job is becoming all the more important. Matching creative development companies with powerful game publishers, as producers do, is what has so far contributed to the success that the game industry enjoys today.

FOR MORE INFORMATION

ORGANIZATIONS

International Game Developers Association (IGDA)
870 Market Street, Suite 1181
San Francisco, CA 94102-3002

(415) 738-2104

Web Site: http://www.igda.org

> IGDA is a nonprofit organization whose members are game-development professionals. In addition to providing general information about game development, the site allows you to register to become a member. Association membership offers you access to other members, meetings, and more.

Producers Guild of America

8530 Wilshire Boulevard, Suite 450

Beverly Hills, CA 90211

(310) 358-9020

Web site: http://www.producersguild.org

> The Producers Guild of America is an organization dedicated to production excellence in motion pictures, television, and new media, which includes video games. Here you will find people with production experience who can help you with your career.

WEB SITES

Answers.com: Game Producer

http://www.answers.com/topic/game-producer

> Answers.com is a general information site that is both authoritative and comprehensive. The Game Producer page on the Web site defines what a game producer is and describes the job's functions and responsibilities in detail. Links to other sites on game production are also included.

Blue Sky Resumes: Video Game Producer Resume

http://www.blueskyresumes.com/resume_sample_06.html

> This Web page provides sample résumés for various industries and offers a look at a sample résumé for someone wanting to become a game producer.

Elektrogames: The Game Production Company
http://www.elektrogames.com

This is the official Web site for the company Elektrogames. Here you can see exactly what a game production company does as well as gain information on its projects and clients. Also available is a contact page should you wish to request additional information from the company itself.

Gamasutra.com
http://www.gamasutra.com

This all-encompassing site is a haven for game enthusiasts. Its features include general video game articles, information, forums, and job boards, as well as a wealth of information specific to video game production.

Phoenix Game Studio
http://www.phoenix-gamestudios.com

Based in Malaysia, this production company produces games for standard consoles such as Xbox and PlayStation, and for mobile phones. Phoenix is a small firm, but is on the cutting edge of the industry. Novices can learn a great deal from this dynamic company.

BOOKS

Adams, Ernest. *Break into the Game Industry: How to Get a Job Making Video Games.* New York, NY: McGraw Hill/Osborne, 2003.
Do you want to know what the typical résumé of a game producer looks like? Or learn what skills to develop to increase your chances for successfully landing a job? This book provides the answers. Filled with specific and practical information, it is indispensable for those on the verge of hunting for a producer job.

Cohen, Judith Love. *You Can Be a Woman Video Game Producer.* Marina del Rey, CA: Cascade Press, Inc., 2005.
Part of a series of career books instructing young women, this title provides information for those interested in game design and shows how women are a major part of this burgeoning industry.

Gershenfeld, Alan, et al. *Game Plan: The Insider's Guide to Breaking In and Succeeding in the Computer and Video Game Business.* New York, NY: St. Martins Press, 2003.
If you're looking for a job in game production, you should start with this book. Though it covers the game industry in general, it offers excellent advice on how to interview, gives tips on résumé writing, and lists the types of credentials that are helpful in securing a job.

Iris, Dan. *The Game Producer's Handbook.* New York, NY: Muska & Lipman, 2005.
An indispensable reference for both the novice and expert game designer. For the beginner, it gives advice on how to succeed in a changing industry. For the veteran game designer, the book offers help to refine his or her skills.

Mencher, Marc. *Get in the Game: Careers in the Game Industry.* Berkeley, CA: New Riders, 2002.
One of the most respected professionals in the industry provides detailed information on how to secure a game production job. Mencher also teaches readers how to launch their careers, from writing the perfect resume to what to say during an interview.

7

TESTER

For someone who likes to play video games, the position of game tester is a dream job. Game testers, basically, are paid to play video games. You may be thinking: What's the catch? There is no catch. Game testers, literally, get paid for doing what they love.

Before shipping their products to stores and selling them to

Though it seems like game testers have it easy, sitting around playing video games all day, testing any particular aspect of a game can go on for hours, if not days. Game testers, such as these at a pre-launch party at the game company Electronic Arts, are critical in making sure customers get what they pay for: a glitch-free gaming experience.

customers, companies must ensure that they are glitch-free and of expected quality. Because video games are relatively complex products, with all sorts of computer code written into them, many things could go wrong. This is why game testers are so important. They play the games over and over again to make sure that there are no problems with the products before they are sold to eager players.

Game testing is fun, but it is foremost a job. Though some testing involves playing the game to analyze its enjoyability, testers primarily look for specific potential problems.

There are three kinds of game testing: bug testing, configuration testing, and game play testing and tuning. Bug testing is fairly self explanatory: You are looking for bugs, or general glitches, in the game. When you come across a bug, you try to figure out what caused the problem. This involves going back and retracing your steps. Let's say the bug is that the game is crashing. Did the crash occur when the quarterback, for example, passed the ball to the wide receiver? If so, the tester tries again to have the quarterback pass the ball to the wide receiver. If the game crashes again, this specific action is likely the cause. The tester then records the problem so it can be analyzed and fixed.

Configuration testing makes sure the game works across all platforms. In other words, does the game work on the Xbox platform the same way it works on PlayStation 2? Are there certain problems that happen on PlayStation 2 that don't occur when playing the game on Xbox? The configuration tester looks for these discrepancies.

Last, but definitely not least, is game play testing and tuning. If you like playing video games, which is probably the case if you are reading this book, you may like the sound of this game testing position the most. Game play testing and tuning basically involves seeing if the game is enjoyable. With bug testing and configuration testing, you are usually

For game testers, constantly checking for glitches can mean hours upon hours behind the controller. Professional testers must be able to endure sitting down staring at a screen for long stretches of time. Though playing games over and over may sound like a dream job, your endurance may be what is put to the test.

playing certain parts of a game over and over, looking for specific problems. With testing and tuning, you are just playing the game as you wish, which makes this job the most fun.

Education and Training

The next time your mom tells you that you are wasting time playing video games, tell her that video games are providing you with valuable career experience. Why? Well, the experience necessary for becoming a game tester is, you guessed it, playing video games. Companies look for people who are already knowledgeable on the subject. There are, however, a few additional requirements.

You should have a good attention to detail. This is necessary in order to track the origins of any problems that occur. Good communication skills are also a must since you will have to explain the nature of any bugs to programmers. Additionally, patience is a virtue since you will likely encounter continuing problems with the games you play. You should not get frustrated if a game constantly crashes since these are the types of things you will be paid to look for. Finally, though not necessary, it is to your advantage if you have some programming skills. If you do come face to face with a glitch, programming knowledge will help you understand the problem better and explain it to your team more clearly.

Salary

The salary for game testers is not as high as in other sectors of the gaming industry, but do not despair. Testing is a great

While game testing involves looking for program glitches, the job of reviewing games for harmful content has become a serious matter over the past few years. Patricia Vance *(right)*, president of the Entertainment Software Rating Board, is responsible for judging a game's appropriateness for children based on its violence, sexual content, and language.

Breaking In

For Jon Gramlich of Monolith Productions, breaking into the game industry as a tester was somewhat accidental. Jon, as profiled in *Break into the Game Industry*, was sending out résumés left and right looking for a computer programming job. None of the companies he interviewed with were a perfect match. Every one was very conservative and wanted someone with more experience. Jon grew desperate and began sending résumés to any company he could find.

Soon after, he landed an interview with GT Interactive. He had no idea it was a video game company, so he was a bit surprised when he saw posters for the games *Wolfenstein 3-D* and *Doom II* on the walls. GT Interactive was looking for someone to set up a virtual bulletin board for technical support and customer service inquiries. Jon had some experience in setting up bulletin boards in the past, and after only a few minutes in the interview, he got the job. Oh, and a large portion of Jon's job, the interviewer told him, would be spent testing games. Jon had no problem with that!

way to get your foot in the door of the business, and from there, there is a lot of potential for you to rise. Game testing is often freelance work, and pay is therefore by the hour. In general, bug testers and game play testers earn $7 to $12 an hour. Configuration testers earn a little more, about $12 to $20 an hour. There is an upside to this, though. As a game comes closer to launch, testers generally work more hours, sometimes even seven days a week. There's potential to make a lot of money if you don't mind playing video games all day long!

Outlook

Game testing is becoming less often an entry-level job and is gaining more respect within the industry. With the game industry now larger than the movie business, and individual games sometimes making more money than Hollywood blockbusters, it is critical that games have no glitches. The average game tester today is twenty-nine years old, and a third are women. From these statistics, it is clear that testing is a job that is becoming more and more respectable.

FOR MORE INFORMATION

WEB SITES

Answers.com: Computer Game Tester
http://www.answers.com/topic/computer-game-tester

An extremely practical reference for video game testing. Here you will find the official definition of video game tester and a detailed list of job responsibilities, as well as links to useful outside Web pages.

GameBriefs.com
http://www.gamebriefs.com

A Web site that offers concise information about the most popular titles and trends in the video and computer gaming industry.

GameStudies.org
http://www.gamestudies.org

GameStudies.org is an online academic journal dedicated to studying developments and trends in the gaming industry.

GameTester.com
http://www.gamestester.com

Do you want to know more about being a game tester? This site is the place to go. It features articles on the industry in general, including how to get your foot in the door and what it is like to work as a game tester for a big company.

Kidzworld.com: Video Game Tester
http://www.kidzworld.com/site/p1904.htm

Kidzworld.com features fun things for kids. On its Video Game Tester page, you will find all the information you need about the job, including what a video game tester does, how to become a video game tester, and how much the job pays.

NPR.org: Day in the Work Life: Video Game Tester
http://soundmoney.publicradio.org/display/web/2005/01/29/ditwl

This National Public Radio Web page offers an audio clip of an interview with a game tester. The interview gives a candid view of the career as well as some of its benefits and drawbacks.

Sloperama.com: Working as a Game Tester
http://www.sloperama.com/advice/lesson5.html

This Web site offers extremely honest advice about game testing, including both the benefits and pitfalls of the job.

WorthPlaying.com
http://www.worthplaying.com

This site covers all the latest games and gives you an idea of whether the game is worth your time and money. This is a particularly useful site for game testers since you can find out what's hot and the types of games that succeed in the market.

PERIODICALS

Computer Games
65 Millet Street, Suite 203
Richmond, VT 05477
(802) 434-3060
Web site: http://www.cgonline.com

This print and online magazine includes articles and reviews about the latest games on the market and is a great resource to stay on top of the industry trends.

Game Informer
724 North 1st Street, 4th Floor
Minneapolis, MN 55401
(612) 486-6100
Web site: http://www.gameinformer.com

This leading video game publication is required reading for anyone interested in keeping up with the latest video games on the market.

ONLINE GAME RENTAL ENTREPRENEUR

As further evidence that the video game business is becoming more and more like the movie industry, rentals of video games are becoming as popular as movie rentals. And if you have more than a few video games in your library, which you probably do if you are an avid gamer, you might have what you need to start a hot new business: online video game rentals. Here is how it works: You create a library of games that your customers can choose to rent. This collection can be the games you currently have, or you can buy new ones to expand your selection. Once you have this library, your customers can rent a game at a time for a monthly subscription fee, which is usually around $15. Once your customer subscribes and chooses a game, you mail it to him or her. The customer can keep the game for as long as he or she wants, but will only be able to rent another when the first is returned. Sounds simple, right? Well, it is. This rental system is based on that of a company called Netflix, which is a very popular online movie rental business.

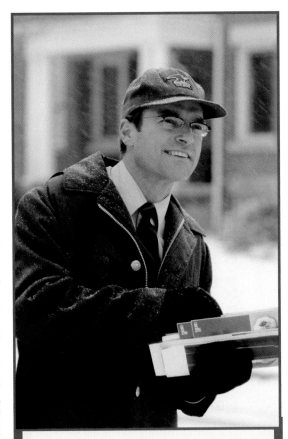

Did you ever think that the mailman could be your business partner? Online game rental entrepreneurs use the postal service to deliver video games to customers. Whenever someone wants to rent a game, all he or she has to do is visit your Web site to place an order.

You might be asking, How do I start? This is the hardest part. To begin, you are going to need a little money and a lot of guts. Starting your own business is never easy, but the payoff can be extraordinary.

As mentioned before, you will need a library of games from which your customers can rent. You can start small with just a handful of games. You might already have these in your personal library. Your customers will probably eventually want a wider pool of games from which to choose, though. So as you become more successful, you should add more and more games and multiple copies of each title to your ever-expanding selection.

You are also going to need a Web site. This is where you will conduct all your business. Your customers will place their orders through the site, so the portal is going to have to be pretty advanced. You may need to hire a professional to set up the site so that it can accept credit card orders, remember individual customers and their order history, and maintain a list of video games they select to rent in the future.

Finally, you are going to need envelopes. If you have an online video game rental business, the United States Postal Service will become one of your main business partners, since each game transaction is sent through the mail. Most online rental businesses deliver their games in a durable envelope that also serves as a prepaid return

If you are not familiar with Web design, you may need to have a professional help you develop your site. Your site will need to be able to process credit cards since it is a rental business. It will also need to have a database to store customer information, such as which games the customer has yet to return.

envelope. All the customer needs to do to return the game is drop it in a mailbox because the postage is prepaid by you. You will have to have these envelopes specially printed. You will also have to talk to your local post office about setting up a business mail account that allows you to send prepaid mail. (Don't worry—there are links to more information about this at the end of the chapter.)

Don't be fooled into thinking that setting up your own business is as easy as one, two, three. It is a big deal. Be sure to do a lot of research before you begin. A good book to pick up is *Start Your Own Business* by Rieva Lesonsky. This title covers many of the technical steps you need to consider before taking the plunge, such as setting up a bank account and making sure you are conducting business in a legal manner. Once you do your research, however, you will be on your way to becoming an entrepreneur.

Education and Training

A good thing about being an entrepreneur is that you are your own boss. One of the things this means is that no one else judges whether you are qualified for the job. Anyone, regardless of whether he or she has any history in the gaming industry, can be an online game rental business entrepreneur.

However, just because you don't have to have any official credentials does not mean you don't need certain skills for the job. To run your own business, you need to have patience. Most businesses don't earn money in the first few months or even years. You should have the ability to stick it out and not quit before your profits are realized. You will also need to pay a great attention to detail. As a business owner, you will be working with a lot of specifics, such as customer databases and money calculations. If you are not exact with these important aspects of your business, serious

The Three Steps to Success

Since starting a game rental business is a job that requires you to do all the work without any help from a boss or coworkers, it is important to understand three major steps involved in launching your business successfully:

Design your Web site. First you will need to purchase a URL, or Web site address. This will be the URL of your Web site, so make sure the name is catchy, cool, and informative. You can do a search for available URLs and purchase one at GoDaddy.com, a URL seller. Then you may want to work with a Web designer. Web designers are people who design the look and functionality of Web sites. For your business, you are going to need a Web site that has a shopping cart where orders can be placed and can accept credit cards. To find a good Web designer, search for "Web designer" on Google.com or another search engine.

Purchase inventory. To have a game rental business, of course you will need games. This requires some investment on your end. You do not have to spend a lot of money, however. You can start with just the few games you might already own and purchase

(continued on following page)

(continued from previous page)

more as you begin to make some money. Eventually, you will have a full library of all the games you can imagine.

Promote your business. Businesses are rarely successful without being promoted. Send out e-mails to everyone in your e-mail address book. Tell your family and friends, and ask them to spread the word to others as well. You might even want to print up some flyers and hang them around town. One thing is for sure, the more promotion, the better.

problems can occur. Finally, you need to have good communication skills. Successful businesses are seldom created by just one person. You will need the help of other professionals, and this means being able to communicate your vision to them clearly and concisely.

Salary

Another good thing about being your own boss is that you can set your own salary. However, your salary is dependent on how successful your business is. If your business is not making any money, neither will you. A lot of business owners do not take all of the profit from their businesses as salary.

GPlay.com was one of the first online game rental businesses and is a good model for entrepreneurs to study. For a monthly subscription fee, customers can rent a set number of games and do not have to worry about late fees or when they need to return them. GPlay even offers aspiring online rental entrepreneurs help in starting their own businesses.

Instead they reinvest, or put money back into the business, to make it grow. You can also sell your business, just like you would sell a bike or a car. Though you will no longer own it, if the business is successful, you can make a lot of money.

Outlook

There are online video game rental businesses popping up every day, such as GPlay.com and RedOctane.com. Even Blockbuster Video established its own video game rental boutique called Game Rush. This is clear evidence that gamers are fed up with paying $50 or more to purchase each new video game. Why spend that much for one video game when for the same amount of money, you can rent several dozen? Yet, though the business is growing, the competition is stiff. By setting up your own rental business, you run the risk of losing money to the guy next door who established a similar business. There is always a risk in starting your own business, so be sure to research your market and establish a competitive edge.

FOR MORE INFORMATION

ORGANIZATIONS
SCORE
SCORE Association
409 3rd Street SW, 6th Floor
Washington, DC 20024
(800) 634-0245
Web site: http://www.score.org
> SCORE is a nonprofit organization that offers free and confidential advice and training for the formation, growth, and success of small

businesses. The Web site offers an "e-mail for advice" section, information about local chapter offices and workshops, and "how to" articles.

United States Small Business Administration (SBA)

6302 Fairview Road, Suite 300
Charlotte, NC 28210
(800) 827-5722
Web site: http://www.sba.gov

The SBA, a U.S. government organization, provides small businesses with aid, counseling, and assistance. Among other things, its Web site includes information on starting, financing, and managing a business; information on training; a teen business link; and online support.

WEB SITES

Entrepreneur.com: Biz Startups

http://www.entrepreneur.com/bizstartups/0,4235,,00.html

The "Startups" section on this Web site provides all you need to know for the early stages of launching your own business, including how to secure financing, incorporate your business, and develop a successful marketing campaign.

Gamefly.com

http://www.gamefly.com

Gamefly is currently the largest online game rental business. On their Web site, you can see exactly how their business model works and take tips from the most successful player in the field. Make sure to check the site from time to time as they are always inventing new ways to improve their service.

Gameznflix.com

http://www.gameznflix.com

Gameznflix.com is a combination movie and video game rental business. By researching this site, you can learn exactly what strategies work for game rentals and if these strategies are different from those for movie rentals. These tips might be able to help you refine your own business plan.

GPlay.com
http://www.gplay.com
GPlay is an online game rental business. It offers a service that allows you to build your own online rental business using its custom software. Through the link "Build Your Own Online Business," you can speak to a representative to see if this solution works for you.

MovieGameRentals.com
http://www.moviegamerentals.com/video-games-rentals.htm
This site compares the different game rental services available. In addition to rating them based on their quality of service, price, and performance, it provides links to a wealth of online rental businesses.

Netflix
http://www.netflix.com
Netflix is the online movie rental business that pioneered the mailed movies model. Soon after Netflix debuted, online game rental businesses started appearing. On this site, you can learn exactly how Netflix works and use this information to build and enhance your own online game rental business.

United States Postal Service
http://www.usps.com
The United States Postal Service Web site provides all the information you need to set up a business mail account for your online game rental business.

BOOKS

Adams, Terry, and Rob Adams. *Start Your Own Mail Order Business: Your Step-by-Step Guide to Success.* (Entrepreneur Magazine's Startup). Irvine, CA: Entrepreneur Press, 2003.

Though there are many types of mail order businesses, they all share certain business practices and strategies. This book will show you the tricks of the trade and provide advice from other similar businesses.

Levinson, Jay Conrad. *Guerrilla Marketing: Secrets for Making Big Profits from Your Small Business*. Boston, MA: Houghton Mifflin, 1998.
Success in small business is often related to how aggressively you market your goods and services. This book teaches how to market your business through nontraditional media, which will allow you to stand out and gain customers.

Purdy, Warren G. *The Service Business Planning Guide: The Complete Handbook for Creating a Winning Business Plan for Any Service Company*. New York, NY: Inc. Business Resources, 1996.
Before starting your online rental business, you must have a business plan. This book helps you outline your business on paper and focus its strategies and goals.

Strauss, Steven D. *The Small Business Bible: Everything You Need to Know to Succeed in Your Small Business*. Hoboken, NJ: John Wiley & Sons, Inc., 2004.
A handy reference not only at the startup phase of your business, but through every step of the life of your company.

Tyson, Eric. *Small Business for Dummies*. 2nd ed. Hoboken, NJ: John Wiley & Sons, Inc., 2003.
This is a comprehensible introduction to the fundamentals of starting a successful business. There are many steps in the beginning phases of a business, and this book walks you through to make sure you do everything correctly from the start.

9

RETAIL STORE SALESPERSON

Do you know where you will find some of the most knowledgeable people in the gaming industry? It is not necessarily in the top management positions at the leading game manufacturing companies. Nor is it always in creative or production jobs at the most cutting-edge game production companies. The most informed people in the industry are often working in the stores where the games are bought.

Game store salespeople, such as this one *(right)* who works at the Virgin Megastore in London, are often the most knowledgeable and enthusiastic game professionals. They have to be. There are countless customers who need information and want to know about the hottest games.

If you walk into any store that sells video games and video game equipment, you will notice that the salespeople are often both enthusiastic and eager to assist you with any of your questions. The reason for this is that store managers look to hire a sales team that is able to answer customer questions and offer information about the latest games on the market. Do you know a lot about video games? Are you on the cutting edge of industry trends? Are you aware of the hottest games that companies will be putting out in the next couple of years? If so, you might fit right in at a retail store.

The first and primary aspect of a salesperson's job is, of course, selling games. This means you will likely be working with a cash register and ringing up dozens, or even hundreds, of games a day. Working the cash register is often a fast-paced and detail-oriented responsibility. You will be dealing with money, so you will have to account for every penny that goes into or comes out of the register. There will be times when a hot game hits the market and it seems like half the world is on line in your store with that game in hand. In such situations, salespeople have to keep calm, alert, and focused.

The second function of the job, sharing your knowledge with customers, is more fun, but no less important, than handling the register. In fact, it may be even more important since getting people to the cash register in the first place sometimes requires convincing them to buy the game. The way you influence people to make a purchase is by informing them about the product. This is where you can work your magic. Salespeople often walk around the store and interact with customers. If you see a customer who looks puzzled or curious about a particular product, you may strike up a

Convincing people to buy video games sometimes takes more than informing them about the products. Often, the quickest way to sell a game is simply to leave customers alone to test it for themselves. In this video game store in Wilsonville, Oregon, two kids enjoy playing the latest games on the in-store console.

conversation. Often, customers do not like to be bothered, so being a successful salesperson involves being able to win over your customers. This requires good interpersonal skills.

Education and Training

The most important requirement for a job as a video game store salesperson is an intense interest in video games. This may sound obvious, but if you don't have a strong curiosity for the latest products on the market, you may have trouble keeping pace with your customers and fellow salespeople. Be sure to keep up to date with the industry magazines, such as *PC Gamer*; game Web sites, such as GamePro.com; and video gaming message boards.

Also useful, but not always necessary, is previous retail sales experience and knowledge about working a cash register. Familiarity with these two things is helpful because it shows that you understand what is involved in running a successful retail operation.

Salary

Since a salesperson job at a video game store is often an entry-level position, game retail outlets, for the most part, pay by the hour. First-time game store salespeople usually earn minimum wage (in 2005, $5.15 to $7.35 an hour, depending on the state). Someone with a couple of years' experience earns about $12 an hour. You can expect to be paid one and a half times your hourly wage for overtime

With so many video games on the market, the best way to succeed as a game store salesperson is to be informed about all the latest products. Customers are faced with an endless selection of titles, so it is important to know each game well.

hours (such as when a new game comes out and in December before the holidays). After you have some experience, you can work your way up to manager. With the promotion, your salary would naturally increase, and instead of an hourly wage, you would likely be paid an annual salary, which would be around $37,000 per year.

Outlook

Becoming a video game retail salesperson is a great way to launch a career in the video game industry. Not only will you become more knowledgeable by working with a group of people with the same interest as you, but you will also gain valuable experience. This experience can help launch you into managing a video game retail outlet or even someday owning your own store.

FOR MORE INFORMATION

ORGANIZATIONS

National Association of Sales Professionals (NASP)
11000 North 130th Place
Scottsdale, AZ 85259
(480) 951-4311
Web site: http://www.nasp.com
>The NASP is an organization devoted to bringing sales professionals together to network and learn from one another's experiences. The organization's Web site offers a listing of jobs as well as membership information.

Retail Alberta
14907 - 111 Avenue
Edmonton, AB T5M 2P6
Canada
(800) 758-9840 or (403) 453-1192
Web site: http://www.retailalberta.ca
>An association that provides support, services, and benefits in order to enhance the professionalism, efficiency, and profitability of its members' businesses. The Web site includes links to other related Canadian organizations. Similar associations exist in other Canadian provinces.

Retail Council of Canada (RCC)
1255 Bay Street, Suite 800
Toronto, ON M5R 2A9
Canada
(888) 373-8245 or (416) 922-6678
Web site: http://www.retailcouncil.org
RCC advances and protects the interests of the Canadian retail industry, using advocacy, research, and education to enhance the opportunity of retail success. Its members include department stores, mass merchants, specialty chains, independent stores, and online sellers.

WEB SITES

About.com: Career Planning: Retail Salesperson
http://careerplanning.about.com/od/occupations/p/retail_sales.htm
This Web page provides all the information you need to become a retail salesperson. From the job description and employment facts to related articles, the site is a quick and easy resource.

GameStop.com
http://www.gamestop.com
GameStop is a chain of game stores owned by the bookseller Barnes & Noble, Inc. On GameStop's Web site, you can find links to its retail stores, which include the contact information necessary to apply for a job at one of its outlets.

The Princeton Review: Career Profiles: Retail Salesperson
http://www.princetonreview.com/cte/profiles/dayInLife.asp?careerID=138
The Princeton Review is the authority on education and careers, and its retail salesperson page is an informative look into the career. The site offers information on a salesperson's daily work-day as well as requirements for the profession and possible internships.

U.S. Department of Labor: Bureau of Labor Statistics: Retail Salespersons
http://www.bls.gov/oco/ocos121.htm
This site from the U.S. Department of Labor offers unvarnished information about the sales industry. Included is specific information about what the work entails, qualifications, working conditions, required skills and training, job outlook, earning potential, and related occupations.

BOOKS

Gitomer, Jeffrey. *The Little Red Book of Selling: 12.5 Principles of Sales Greatness.* Austin, TX: Bard Press, 2004.
This offbeat book by the author of *The Sales Bible* takes a fun and energetic approach to teaching its readers how to become successful salespeople. In a colorful format with many humorous illustrations, this book is both informative and entertaining.

Hopkins, Tom, and Laura Laaman. *The Certifiable Salesperson: The Ultimate Guide to Help Any Salesperson Go Crazy with Unprecedented Sales.* Hoboken, NJ: John Wiley & Sons, Inc., 2002.
If you have decided that sales is the profession for you, this book is a great start to learning about how to succeed. It teaches you how to increase your sales by changing your voice, wardrobe, and conversation habits.

Schiffman, Stephen. *The 25 Sales Habits of Highly Successful Salespeople.* Avon, MA: Adams Media Corporation, 1994.
This bestseller provides practical advice on what works in the sales world. Analyzing twenty-five practices successful salespeople use, this book covers such topics as asking the right questions, engaging your customer, and taking a leadership role in a sale.

10

RETAIL STORE OWNER

If you like sales but don't like the idea of working for an employer (as you would if you were a video game store salesperson), you might want to think about opening a video game retail store of your own. With the growing popularity of video games, it makes sense that video game stores are also growing more successful. Video game retail stores,

It can be a challenging venture to run a retail store. Video game stores are especially busy around the holidays and whenever a new product hits the market, such as Sony's PlayStation Portable (PSP). Here, a Sony executive *(right)* sells the first PSP at the product launch in New York City on March 23, 2005.

such as GameStop, which is owned by the bookstore chain Barnes & Noble, are popping up left and right.

Video game stores sell video games. You might be saying, "of course video game stores sell video games." This seems like an obvious statement, but it is necessary to remember this is the key to your success, or your business plan, as a store owner. A lot of different stores sell video games. Retailers such as Target and Wal-Mart sell tons of video games, and they likely sell them for a lower price than what you will be able to offer. The difference is that Target and Wal-Mart sell a lot of other things, too, from bath towels to tiki torches. That you sell only video games is a big plus to the person who knows that he wants a new video game and doesn't want to walk through aisles and aisles of other products that he couldn't care less about. He wants to browse video games and nothing but video games. Which store do you think he will choose? You're right; probably yours.

There is a saying in the real estate business that the three most important things to consider are location, location, location. A high-traffic area, such as this street, is an example of a good place to set up shop. Your store will get the exposure it needs and, with so many people passing by every day, you will no doubt have lots of customers.

Now that you have your business idea—to launch a store that sells only video games and related products—you need to decide on a location. Do you know of an area where there is a good market for a video game store? You will want to look for a place where there is a large customer base and little

LARA CROFT·TOMB RAIDER·THE CRADLE OF LIFE

competition from other retailers. You will also want to look for a high-traffic location, where a lot of people will pass by your store. The more people who pass by, the more people who will come in and buy your merchandise.

The next step is to create your business plan. There are many software programs available that will help you do this in a professional manner. A professional-looking business plan is necessary in case you need to approach a bank for a loan to get your business started. Banks frequently lend entrepreneurs money to buy inventory—in your case, video games and related products. The loan could also be used to pay the rent for your storefront and other expenses like insurance, accounting, and legal fees. Once you start making money, you pay the loan back to the bank with interest.

Education and Training

Like the other careers covered in this book, being a store owner is not as hard as it may seem. Unlike the other careers mentioned, however, there are certain qualities you

Video game companies often allow other companies to license, or use, a video game's name on other products, such as action figures and comic books. Retail store entrepreneurs can benefit from selling these game-related products, such the ones seen here, related to *Lara Croft Tomb Raider: The Cradle of Life*.

absolutely must have to be successful. This advice is not meant to discourage you, but if you feel that you do not have these traits, or are not able to acquire them, you are probably better off choosing a career to which you are better suited.

First, you need to be a people person. Just because you are starting a business yourself doesn't mean that no one else will be involved. You must be able to get along with others, such as bankers, lawyers, accountants, and any employees you might hire.

Second, you must be detail oriented. There are a lot of particulars that come with starting a business—everything from the research of your market to the fine print in contracts. You will need to be able to juggle all these details because one minor error could create major problems down the road.

Finally, you should be an optimist. An optimist, even in tough times, believes that things will turn out well. You may come across some difficult periods in your business experience, so an optimistic attitude is crucial in order to weather these storms.

Salary

As with the online game rental business, a game store owner's salary is completely up to how well the business does. As the owner, you are the boss, so you can set your own salary. Your salary, however, depends on how much money your business makes. If your business is losing money, you will not be able to pay yourself a hefty income.

As mentioned in the online game rental business chapter, many business owners take modest paychecks for themselves and reinvest some of their profits back into the business. By doing this, they allow their businesses to grow, which, down the line, potentially produces more profits and possibly larger paychecks.

Outlook

The video game business is growing at a rapid pace. Therefore, the market for video game retailers is likewise expanding. This is a good sign. However, the more video game retailers there are as a result of this growing market, the more competition there is for you. When there is so much competition that it is hard to be successful, the market is what is called saturated. A saturated market allows little or no room for newcomers, the same way a saturated sponge can absorb little or no additional water. This will likely happen in the coming years. As an entrepreneur, it is your job to be able to predict when the market will become saturated and start your business before this happens.

FOR MORE INFORMATION

ORGANIZATIONS

Interactive Entertainment Merchants Association (IEMA)
IEMA/Crest Group
64 Danbury Road, Suite 700
Wilton, CT 06897-4406
(203) 761-6180
Web site: http://www.iema.org
> IEMA is the only U.S. nonprofit trade association dedicated to serving the business interests of retailers that sell interactive entertainment software. Check its Web site for news, services, and events.

National Retail Federation (NRF)
325 7th Street NW, Suite 1100
Washington, DC 20004
(800) NRF-HOW2 (673-4692)
Web site: http://www.nrf.com
> The NRF is the world's largest retail association. Its site provides a wealth of information from government regulations to retail store magazines. If you are interested in opening a video game retail store, this is the place to begin.

The Retail Owners Institute
c/o Outcalt & Johnson: Retail Strategists, LLC
1326 Fifth Avenue, Suite 620
Seattle, WA 98101
(800) 499-7531
Web site: http://www.retailowner.com

A perfect source for those who want to go into the retail industry. The Web site offers valuable information on how to run a success- ful retail business and provides a list of software, articles, and other resources related to the industry.

WEB SITES

About.com: Retail Industry
http://retailindustry.about.com
This page on About.com provides general information about the industry, which you can use for market research. Explaining the retail environment today, this site also analyzes large retail compa- nies such as Wal-Mart, Costco, and Walgreens. You can use this information to refine your own business plan.

EB Games
http://www.ebgames.com/ebx/default.asp#
EB Games is a retail outlet much like GameStop. Though EB Games and GameStop are large, multistate chain stores, they will be your competition. Use the Store Locator feature on this site to pinpoint EB Games store locations. You can use this information to help determine where you want to locate your own business.

Wikipedia.org: Top Selling Video Games
http://en.wikipedia.org/wiki/List_of_best_selling_video_games
This site lists the top-selling video games. As a video game retail store owner, this list will become very important to you since you will want to stock popular games, as well as track such industry trends.

BOOKS

Corinna, Dean. *Inspired Retail Space: Attract Customers, Build Branding, Increase Volume.* Gloucester, MA: Rockport Publishers, 2005. Appearance is very important in retail business. Without a well- laid-out store, you may not attract as many customers as you could otherwise. This book offers advice on how to design your retail space to its best advantage.

Dion, Jim, and Ted Topping. *Start and Run a Profitable Retail Business.* Bellingham, WA: Self-Counsel Press, 2000.
This book is a soup-to-nuts guide for starting a retail business. Topics include the basics of retail, merchandising, buying inventory, hiring personnel, tracking inventory, using computer technology, and customer service.

Falk, Edgar A. *1,001 Ideas to Create Retail Excitement, Revised Edition.* New York, NY: Prentice Hall Press, 2003.
It is one thing to start a retail business; it is entirely another to make it successful. This book focuses on ways you can make your business as profitable as possible by such practices as paying attention to your product and focusing on customer service.

Heard, Geoffrey, and Gordon Wolf. *Success in Store: How to Start or Buy a Retail Business, Enjoy Running It and Make Money.* Mentone, Australia: Worsley Press, 2003.
If you do not want to start your retail store from scratch, you could buy an existing one. This book guides you through the advantages and disadvantages of both options.

Taylor, Don. *Up Against the Wal-Marts: How Your Business Can Prosper in the Shadow of the Retail Giants.* New York, NY: American Management Association, 1996.
As a video game retailer, your biggest competitor may very well be the retail behemoth Wal-Mart or similar chain stores. This book offers advice on how to stand out in the shadow of such retail giants by using low-cost promotion strategies.

11

MARKETING MANAGER

Game promotion has become one of the most important, and innovative, sectors of the industry, and there is a constant search for new ways to get games into the hands of consumers.

The job of a marketing manager is to advertise and sell new products. In the past, advertising was traditionally a simple and direct process, which

involved either buying television commercial time or taking out an ad in a print magazine to promote a particular product. Today, however, with the Internet and a new generation of media-savvy kids, video game companies are looking for inventive ways to alert the public about their products.

A marketing manager is responsible for a number of different types of promotion, including product designs, store displays, ad campaigns, licensing, and trade shows. Let's take a look at each in detail.

There is a well-known saying, don't judge a book by its cover. However, marketing managers know that gamers certainly do judge a game by its cover and packaging. Coordinating with artists and the game developers themselves, marketing managers help develop the concept and theme for a game's packaging so that consumers will want to pick the game up and bring it home.

Store displays are actually a part of packaging. Have you ever seen a new game set up in its own cardboard rack, maybe at the entrance of a store? These displays are designed

It is a marketing manager's responsibility to make sure that a game's packaging is the best it can be. This packaging for *L.A. Rush*, a car racing game, captures the feel of this fast-paced, dynamic title. Vibrant packaging helps sell video games because it gives customers a sense of the game's excitement.

One way marketing managers promote new products is by arranging launch parties, such as this one for the PlayStation Portable gaming console. Gatherings such as these often attract industry professionals, gaming enthusiasts, and even celebrities. The game companies then get more promotion in the form of press when the news media arrive to cover the event.

to grab your attention before anything else does. The marketing manager decides which games should be displayed in this fashion. She also helps with the design of the displays.

We tend to think of ad campaigns as a series of advertising on TV, in magazines, on billboards, etc. And though the video game industry still promotes its products this way, the Internet has spawned innovative and grassroots methods for getting word about new products out to the public. As a marketing manager, you will spearhead additional modes of advertising, such as through Internet chat rooms, direct-mail

Marketing managers are always looking to use their talents to set up creative and inventive promotional campaigns that will set a game apart from the crowd. Here, Darth Vader and storm troopers stand in New York City's Times Square to launch *Star Wars Battlefront II*.

campaigns, and launch parties. Your responsibility in this job, however, will be to think up fresh ways to advertise, which will allow you to put your creativity to work.

A new area of the gaming industry is licensing. Licensing is when one company allows another company to sell its products in different form or area of the world. For example, when J. K. Rowling wrote the Harry Potter books, she, along with her agent and publisher, allowed the Warner Bros. movie studio to turn the books into a series of movies. In other words, they licensed the movie rights to Warner Bros. Video game companies make similar licensing agreements. A game company may license the rights to, let's say, *Halo* to a book publisher to turn the game concept into a novel or strategy guide. The game company may even license a game—as Microsoft, *Halo*'s creator, recently did—to be made into a movie. Licensing games is a great way to promote a company's products and make additional money.

Finally, marketing managers are involved in game trade shows. Trade shows, which usually happen once a year, are where all the companies in the video game industry display their products to their peers. One of the largest video game trade shows is called the Electronic Entertainment Expo (E^3) and is held annually in May. Marketing managers will decide such things as what the company's booth at the show will look like and in which section it will be placed, depending on the type of video games the company is promoting.

Licensing is a new frontier in the video game industry. Game experts see the money-making potential in teaming up with other media industries such as book publishing and film. *Harry Potter and the Prisoner of Azkaban* was one such licensing success; the Harry Potter tale was also made into a movie and a video game.

Education and Training

Marketing manager is not an entry-level job. You will likely need to gain experience in marketing first by starting out as an assistant to a marketing manager. Unless you already have experience in the marketing department of a gaming company, you will likely start at this level.

Creativity is one important skill you should have. Promoting and marketing a game often involve as much ingenuity as creating the game itself. Every day, consumers are bombarded by all sorts of advertising. Companies want and need their products to stand out from the crowd.

Salary

Your salary in the marketing department of a video game company will, of course, vary depending on your experience. A marketing assistant can make anywhere from $30,000 to $35,000 a year. As a marketing manager, you can expect to make anywhere from $70,000 to $90,000 a year.

Outlook

This is a revolutionary time in the video gaming industry. With new media, such as online magazines, downloadable music, podcasts, and blogs, the new generation of video game buyers is not paying as much attention to the traditional media. Video game companies are now looking to promote their games through these new venues in order to reach younger audiences. It is up to the marketing managers to discover creative ways to get word of these games to the public.

Sean "Hollowtip" Briggs, one of four E^3 champions, plays *America's Army* in Redding, California. The new generation of gamers is more technically sophisticated and media savvy. As a result, marketing managers have to find innovative ways to grab their attention.

FOR MORE INFORMATION

ORGANIZATIONS

American Marketing Association (AMA)
311 South Wacker Drive, Suite 5800
Chicago, IL 60606
(800) AMA-1150 (262-1150)
Web site: http://www.marketingpower.com
   AMA offers information on industry news, marketing practices, and case studies, all of which will help you improve your skills and increase your chances for successfully finding a marketing job.

Business Marketing Association
400 N. Michigan Avenue, 15th Floor
Chicago, IL 60611
(800) 664-4BMA (664-4262) or (312) 822-0005
Web site: http://www.marketing.org
   The Business Marketing Association aids in business-to-business marketing. This is a great place to get an idea of how businesses advertise their products and services and grab one another's attention.

Canadian Marketing Association (CMA)
1 Concorde Gate, Suite 607
Don Mills, ON M3C 3N6
Canada
(416) 391-2362
Web site: http://www.the-cma.org
   CMA is the largest marketing association in Canada, and it is a good starting place for anyone who is interested in finding a marketing job. The Web site includes resources such as education and training, marketing events, and a newsletter.

Marketing Research Association
1344 Silas Deane Highway, Suite 306
Rocky Hill, CT 06067
(860) 257-4008
Web site: http://www.mra-net.org
>The Marketing Research Association is an organization of marketing professionals who help each other with education, networking, and building businesses. It specializes in researching and gathering marketing information that businesses can use to better sell their products.

WEB SITES

MarketingJobs.com
http://www.marketingjobs.com
>On this job board for marketing managers, you can search for a job in video games, or just look at what other marketing jobs are available to try and get a general sense of what the job entails.

Marketing Manager's Plain English Internet Glossary
http://www.jaderiver.com/glossary.htm
>This interesting site offers hundreds of terms that marketing managers use every day, along with easy-to-understand definitions.

Sega of America: Job Board
http://www.recruitforce.com/NA4/ats/careers/jobSearch.jsp?org=SEGAUSA&cws=1
>Sega is one of the leading video game console and game makers. On Sega's job board, you can find out what marketing jobs are available. If you are not yet ready to apply for a position, you can search the job board just to get an idea of what Sega looks for in its employees.

U.S. Department of Labor: Advertising, Marketing, Promotions, Public Relations, and Sales Managers
http://www.bls.gov/oco/ocos020.htm

This site offers a candid profile of the marketing industry and related fields. Included is information about the nature of the work, working conditions, employment statistics, earnings, and job outlook.

BOOKS

Kim, W. Chan, and Renée Mauborgne. *Blue Ocean Strategy: How to Create Uncontested Market Space and Make Competition Irrelevant.* Cambridge, MA: Harvard Business School Press, 2005.
This best-selling book is perfect for marketing professionals. The strategy, which explores new markets, is a good system for marketers searching for an edge over the competition.

Kohler, Chris. *Power-Up: How Japanese Video Games Gave the World an Extra Life.* Indianapolis, IN: Brady Games, 2004.
Do you want to learn about a video game marketing success story? Look at Japanese video games. Their combination of classic Japanese story lines and a unique style have made the games very popular. This book will show you how the Japanese positioned their games to make them successful in the American marketplace.

12

MAGAZINE JOURNALIST

While reading this book, you may have noticed that many jobs in the video game industry require knowledge of computers, such as programmer or designer. Yet others demand that you have good leadership and interpersonal skills, such as video game store owner. You may be saying to yourself that you don't feel that you have the skills

necessary in order to succeed at any of these jobs. Don't worry. There are plenty of jobs out there in which you need neither computer expertise nor the leadership abilities of a business owner. One such career is that of a video game journalist.

If you like to write and play video games, you might want to become a journalist for a video game magazine. Journalists write about video games, but they do much more than just tell readers about the latest products—they follow the video game industry as a whole. This involves playing and reviewing the hottest new games on the market; interviewing industry leaders, such as programmers, designers, and producers; and testing new hardware, such as the latest version of Xbox, the Xbox 360. Who ever said writing was boring?

Now is a great time to get your foot in the door. New magazines are popping up left and right, such as *Game Informer*, *PC Gamer*, *100% Independent PlayStation 2 Magazine*, and *Official Xbox Magazine* to name just a few. Pick up a couple of them at your local bookstore (or look for them free online). There are also online magazines, such as *XBoxAddict* and the

When golf star Tiger Woods appeared at the Times Square Virgin Megastore in New York City to promote *Tiger Woods PGA Tour '06*, many journalists showed up to cover the event. As a video game journalist you are in the perfect position to meet and interview celebrities, industry professionals, and everyday gamers.

Electric Playground. Each of these magazines is looking for edgy new reviews and commentary on the game industry.

The best way to get started is to take a look at some of the magazines' articles and get to know the writing styles of the most frequent contributors. Then try your hand at writing a freelance article or review yourself—writing freelance means that you are writing as a person who is not employed full-time by a magazine. Finally, send your writing to a magazine's editorial office. Print magazines give the addresses of their editorial offices on the masthead page, which is the page that gives all the magazine's corporate information. This is usually the second or third page of the magazine. (Look carefully since the masthead can be easy to miss because the print is so small.) The online magazines usually have a "Contact Us" link somewhere on their main page. Click on the link and sometimes you will find specific instructions on sending in your writing. If a magazine likes your writing and accepts it for publication, then send in another piece. If you get enough of these articles under your belt, a publication might just hire you as a full-time employee.

The other route you can take is simply to send in your résumé. Magazines usually like to see that you have had some writing experience. Did you work on the school paper? Have you ever had any of your writing published? If so, send them copies of your work. If not, you may want to try to write game reviews on game enthusiast message

Journalists often attend press conferences to hear and gather news on gaming events, such as this announcement of Nintendo's new game consoles, Game Boy Micro and Nintendo Revolution. Journalists are among the first people to hear about the latest developments in the industry.

boards or blogs. Then send them printouts of those reviews. This will show the magazine editors that you are not only eager to write about games but that you have an expertise in the field. Otherwise, you can send in your résumé and try to land a job as an assistant to a writer. One great thing about journalism is that it is a good on-the-job training profession. This means that you can go in with little experience and learn from the people around you.

Education and Training

The most important skill you need as a video game magazine journalist is the ability to write so that your reader can understand the topic. The job of the game journalist is not only to write about the latest products and trends but also to profile them in a clear and concise manner. An effective way to learn how to write is to read good writers. Look for writers whose names pop up the most in video game magazines. That their work is often published is a good indication that they are talented. Then compare those writers' styles to those of the less popular writers. Can you see a difference in their styles? What is it? Do you think this difference is what makes their writing better than that of the others?

Also important, of course, is a thorough knowledge of the gaming industry. You should be the first of your friends to know about the latest products and hardware. This means reading up on what's hot and poring over the Internet for the latest trends.

Journalists report on video game equipment and products as well as the games themselves. For example, the Atari Flashback 2 video game console, which was recently rereleased, gets as much attention in a journalist's world as the latest game. The new Atari console was created to pay tribute to the original and allow older players to relive the days of classic games such as *Pong*, *Centipede*, and *Asteroids*.

Salary

Journalists, on average, don't make as much money as others in the industry, but the trade-off is that they have one of the most dynamic jobs in the business. A full-time journalist who is just staring out can expect to make around $26,000 a year. Salary, however, increases with experience. On the high end, journalists with several years of experience can make up to $70,000 a year.

Since the salary for game journalists is relatively low, many supplement their income by doing freelance writing in addition to their day jobs. Freelancers are usually paid by the word, and depending on experience, they can earn anywhere from $0.10 to $1 a word. This may not sound like much, but at $1 a word, an article the length of that one-page essay you wrote for English class could net you anywhere from $250 to $500.

Outlook

Fortunately, with the video game industry doing well, the market for video game magazine journalists is good. With an increasing number of new products, there is more that the magazines have to cover and there are more magazines being launched. With more magazines, there are more employment opportunities for writers. The video game industry does not look like it is going to slow down any time in the near future. Technology is getting better, and games are becoming more innovative by the day. This means that you as a journalist will have a lot of interesting things to write about and will continue to have a lot of attentive readers looking for the hot new products and reviews.

FOR MORE INFORMATION

ORGANIZATIONS

The Canadian Association of Journalists (CAJ)
Algonquin College
1385 Woodroffe Avenue, B224
Ottawa, ON K2G 1V8
Canada
(613) 526-8061
Web site: http://www.caj.ca
> CAJ serves as the national voice of Canadian journalists. It promotes excellence in journalism from all media, including print, television, and radio.

International Game Journalists Association
4563 West 36th Place
Denver, CO 80212
Web site: http://www.igja.org
> This organization provides resources, community, and education for current and aspiring video game journalists. Here you can find news stories, advice, and even jobs in the industry.

Society of Professional Journalists
Eugene S. Pulliam National Journalism Center
3909 North Meridian Street
Indianapolis, IN 46208
(317) 927-8000
Web site: http://www.spj.org

This site is a great first look into a journalist's career. Run by some of the most respected journalists in the world, this organization gives a sense of how the industry works.

WEB SITES

CheatPlanet.com

http://www.cheatplanet.com

Don't worry, you are not doing anything wrong by visiting CheatPlanet.com. It is a Web site that offers tricks to help get ahead in particular games. Someone has to figure out these tricks to put on the Web site, however, and that is where you come in. You can play games, figure out the shortcuts, and then write and report on them to sites such as this one.

GamePro.com

http://www.gamepro.com

GamePro is a video game Web magazine. Since this is an online magazine, articles are continually being updated and new writers are showcasing their articles. This is a good place to get a sense of the writing from some of the leading video game journalists.

BOOKS

Associated Press. *AP Stylebook*. New York, NY: Basic Books, 2004.
This book, commissioned by the Associated Press, is the standard guidebook for journalists. It includes all common journalistic rules, including those for spelling, grammar, and style.

King, Brad, and John Borland. *Dungeons and Dreamers: The Rise of Computer Game Culture from Geek to Chic*. New York, NY: McGraw-Hill/Osborne, 2003.

Probably the longest piece of video game journalism you will read, *Dungeons and Dreamers* is an investigative report into the cultural phenomenon that is video games. Tracking the rise of game impresario Richard Garriott, the authors shed light on how the industry evolved into what it is today. This is a great piece of journalistic reporting.

Levin, Mark. *The Reporter's Notebook: Writing Tools for Student Journalists.* Columbus, NC: Mind-Stretch, 2000.

Perfect for aspiring journalists, *The Reporter's Notebook* teaches students how to record sources, come up with story leads, and keep their punctuation sharp.

PERIODICALS

Computer and Video Games
Web site: http://www.computerandvideogames.com

This industry magazine covers the online hottest trends in the video game business. Included are reports and reviews of the latest games. Read some of these and note how the journalists write. Try to pick up on some of their skills in order to hone your own.

Editor & Publisher
770 Broadway
New York, NY 10003-9595
(800) 336-4380
Web site: http://www.editorandpublisher.com

Editor & Publisher is an industry trade magazine for those in the journalism business. Here you can learn about what is going on in journalism today and get a sense of how the industry works as a whole.

GLOSSARY

analogy A comparison between two things or ideas that are similar in some respects.

business plan A written document that precisely defines your business strategy and identifies your goals.

career Progressive achievement in public, professional, or business life.

communication The process by which verbal or written information is exchanged between individuals.

competition A person or company that produces a product or service that threatens the success of your own in the marketplace.

cutting edge The most advanced or innovative position.

deadline The date or time by which something must be done.

degree A credential from a university or other learning institution given upon completion of a program of study.

editing The process of preparing a video game for presentation by revising and readying content.

experience Practical skill or knowledge gained through direct observation or participation.

freelancer An employee who works on a project-to-project basis without a long-term commitment to any one employer or organization.

functionality The ability of a game or its hardware to work properly.

graphics Visual representations of a game's story line.

innovative Characterized by being creative or new.

interactive Involving a user's orders or responses to affect a game's story line.

inventory The quantity of goods or materials on hand.

managerial Involving the direction or supervision of a person or team, especially relating to business affairs.

market The competitive environment in which a service or product is bought and sold.

marketing The process of promoting, selling, and distributing a product or service.

proficient Skilled in an art, occupation, or branch of knowledge.

retail The business of selling commodities or goods in relatively small quantities directly to the consumer.

salary A fixed payment at regular intervals for professional services.

three-dimensional (3-D) Having the three dimensions of height, width, and depth.

two-dimensional (2-D) Having the two dimensions of height and width.

INDEX

About the Author

Nicholas Croce is an avid video game player and writer. In addition to books, his writing has appeared in the *Bergen News*, the *New York Times*, and the literary journal *Blue Mesa Review*.

Photo Credits

Cover © David McNew/Getty Images; p. 8 © Robyn Beck/AFP/Getty Images; pp., 10, 12, 21, 32, 33, 36, 37, 44, 46, 48, 54, 55, 56, 59, 60, 74, 77, 79, 108, 115, 119, 121, 123, 127, 128, 131, 133 © AP/Wide World Photos; p. 16 by Tahara Anderson; pp. 20, 25, 35 © Indranil Mukherjee/AFP/Getty Images; p. 23 by Tom Forget; p. 49 by Luke Andrews-Hakken; pp. 65, 66 © Christopher J. Morris/Corbis; p. 69 © Patrik Giardino/Cobris; p. 75 © Gail Albert Halaban/Corbis; pp. 84, 91 http://www. gplay.com; p. 85 © LWA-Dann Tardif/Corbis; p. 87 © David Frazier/The Image Works; pp. 96, 101 © Juston Sullivan/Sega Sports/Getty Images; p. 97 © Chris Jackson/Getty Images; p. 99 © Craig Mitchellyer/Getty Images; pp. 105, 106, 118 © Getty Images for Sony; p. 107 © Jon Hicks/Corbis; p. 116 © Business Wire via Getty Images.

Designer: Evelyn Horovicz; Editor: Elizabeth Gavril